Ecstasy and the Rise of the Chemical Generation

Drug users are no longer a mad, bad or immoral minority. Using drugs is normal for the chemical generation, and the drug that defines them is ecstasy. This book about ecstasy users' lives is based on one of the biggest government-funded projects ever undertaken and gives voice to the chemical generation for the first time.

The effects of the manufacture, distribution and use of ecstasy are now being felt across much of the globe. In the UK, where the study was conducted, over fifty per cent of young people use drugs, a quarter of them regularly. The people in this book are ordinary, decent, family-loving people, with normal lives, normal problems and normal aspirations. Through their own words we hear how they first started using ecstasy, how they use it in different ways, why clubbing and raving are so important, how good sex is on ecstasy, how they chill out, how they come down, what problems they have encountered and why they quit.

And what happened to these normal people when they used ecstasy? Nothing. Yet.

This path-breaking book ends by trying to answer the question on the lips of every member of the chemical generation: what are the long-term effects of ecstasy? Because we can't answer them, the authors claim, we are failing in our duty to our children: telling them not to take ecstasy is as alienating as it is pointless.

Richard Hammersley is Professor at the Health and Social Sciences Institute at the University of Essex; **Furzana Khan** is Research and Information Officer for the Glasgow Council for the Voluntary Sector; **Jason Ditton** is Professor of Criminology at the University of Sheffield and Director of the Scottish Centre for Criminology in Glasgow.

Ecstasy and the Rise of the Chemical Generation

Richard Hammersley
University of Essex, UK

Furzana Khan
Glasglow Council for the Voluntary Sector, UK

and

Jason Ditton
University of Sheffield, UK

London and New York

First published 2002
by Routledge
11 New Fetter Lane, London EC4P 4EE

Simultaneously published in the USA and Canada
by Routledge
29 West 35th Street, New York, NY 10001

Routledge is an imprint of the Taylor & Francis Group

Typeset by Expo Holdings, Malaysia
Printed and bound in Great Britain by MPG Books Ltd, Bodmin

British Library Cataloguing in Publication Data
A catalogue record for this book is available from the British Library

Library of Congress Cataloging in Publication Data
A catalog record for this book has been requested

ISBN: 0–415–27040–5 (hbk)
ISBN: 0–415–27041–3 (pbk)

Contents

List of Tables   vii
Preface   ix
Acknowledgements   xi

Chapter One   Introduction—Getting into Ecstasy   1
Getting the Large Sample to Complete the Questionnaires   2
The Small Group that Talked to us on Tape   8
How They got into Ecstasy   19
Getting Others into Ecstasy   25

Chapter Two   Types of Ecstasy User   31
Typologies of Ecstasy Use   32
'Bouncy' E or 'Gouchy' E?   38
Consumption and Tolerance   43
Bingeing   51

Chapter Three   Uses of Ecstasy   59
The Right Mood and the Right Place   60
Clubbing and Raving   67
Sextasy   71
Chilling Out and Coming Down   76

Chapter Four   The Role of Ecstasy   85
Taking Other Drugs   86
The Ecstasy Lifestyle   89
Problems with Ecstasy   99
Quitting Ecstasy   102

Chapter Five   Ecstasy—Impressions and Reality   111
What did They Know?   112
Where are They Now?   116
Where are We Now?   129
Further Reading   139

Appendix   The Information Needs of Ecstasy Users   141

Index   167

List of Tables

Chapter One
1.1   Ecstasy using groups and demographic factors   7

Chapter Two
2.1   Native typologies of levels and patterns of Ecstasy use   35
2.2   Binge frequency and duration by user group   52
2.3   Ecstasy consumption during last binge for those whose binge had lasted several days, by user group   53
2.4   Other drugs taken during last Ecstasy binge   54

Chapter Three
3.1   Sex on Ecstasy and on alcohol   71
3.2   Drinks consumed at last dance event   76
3.3   Substances consumed last time unwell at a dance event   77
3.4   Symptoms experienced last time unwell at a dance event   78

Chapter Four
4.1   Percent using other drugs in year prior to interview   86
4.2   Percent using other drugs used simultaneously with most recent Ecstasy use   87
4.3   Other activities indulged in at least monthly   95
4.4   Purchases made at least monthly   95
4.5   Voting intentions   95
4.6   Offending   96
4.7   Offending: our Ecstasy users and the SCS Ecstasy users   98
4.8   Illegal transactions per week   98
4.9   Average days of illness per year by Ecstasy use pattern   99
4.10 Number reporting symptoms by level of overall drug use   100
4.11 Giving up Ecstasy   103
4.12 Abstaining from Ecstasy   104

Chapter Five
5.1   Percent rating sources of information on Ecstasy   112
5.2   Sources of information on the hazards of Ecstasy   116
5.3   Collapse, oven death   135
5.4   Depression   137

Appendix
A1   Discussion groups   142
A2   Scores for each information source   143
A3   Scores for each information source as "best" source   143
A4   Scores for each information content   147

Preface

As the final touches are being put to this book in the earliest days of the 21st century, the 1990s seem, in retrospect, to be a curious decade. We had fully expected it to be a 'decade of the stimulants' in the late 1980s, and so it turned out to be.[1] Ecstasy, the stimulant which is the focus of this book, had a more curious decade than most drugs. The early 1990s saw a celebratory endorsement of it, as bars across the middle of England closed, and promptly reopened as alcohol-free clubs. By the middle of the decade, alcohol had crept back onto the scene (it has been provocatively suggested that the so-called 'alco-pops' were introduced by the drinks industry not to ensnare children with their sweet taste, but instead to wean Ecstasy users back to more conventional and more dangerous drugs), and unofficial self-organised raves were being broken up more frequently by the police. The tabloids rubbed their hands with glee as club deaths could be laid by them at Ecstasy's door. By the late 1990s, things fell into perspective. The Chemical Generation, or Generation "X", had not migrated into the depressed generation that some had foretold. Hundreds of thousands of doses of Ecstasy are believed to be consumed each week, yet the death rate has not risen, and for many of the deaths associated with Ecstasy (at least in the media) it remains unproven that Ecstasy caused death.

This book reports two of the three separate studies of the use of Ecstasy undertaken by the authors during the 1990s.[2] The major study (which is reported in the five main chapters) compromised quantitative interviews with 229 Ecstasy users, 22 of whom were interviewed qualitatively and in depth. These interviews took place between December 1993 and June 1995. In early 1999, we managed to trace seven of the 22, and re-interviewed them.

In 1994, we studied the information needs of 38 young Ecstasy users. All 38 took part in one of six discussion groups, and 21 of the participants were later interviewed in depth. This is reported in the Appendix.

This book is not aimed exclusively at an academic audience. Quantitative analysis is dealt with lightly in the main text, and more space than would otherwise be appropriate is given to the words of the 22 users we interviewed with a tape-recorder to hand. However, our main quantitative findings have been validated by the scientific peer-review system, and references to these published articles are given where necessary. As we were making final changes to the book, in January 2000, the clubbing magazine Mixmag published the results of a large survey of its readers' drug-using habits.[3] The only major differences we noticed between those findings and the ones in this book were that Ecstasy use seems to have become even more common. For instance, more of the people who replied to the survey had taken ecstasy during the previous month than had taken cannabis. Also, cocaine seemed to becoming more common again.

Two final things. It is a convention amongst researchers working with qualitative data in Scotland to attempt to retain the 'Scottishness' of the original speech, while making it readable elsewhere. This produces tensions between accurate transcribing on the one hand, and avoiding turning Scottish speech into exotic or inarticulate English, rather than as coherent Scottish, on the other. Our solution is to convert most words to standard English spellings, but to retain Scottish grammar and dialect words. We have also retained Glaswegian slang words and specialised drugs slang, some of which have never been dignified with dictionary definitions. We provide working definitions of these as appropriate. Finally, in the text, we refer to Ecstasy like that: with an initial capital even if the word appears in the middle of a sentence. In quoted speech, it is referred to as E or Eccy, several of them as Eees, consuming them as Eeeing and the result of doing so as being Eeed. Simply because that what it sounds like people are saying.

NOTES

1   See Davies, J. and Ditton, J., "The 1990s: Decade of the stimulants?" *British Journal of Addiction*, 1990, 85 (6): 811–813.

2   In 1995, we accompanied a group of 203 young people on a rave package tour to a well-known Mediterranean island, and this is reported in Elliott, L., Morrison, a., Ditton, J., Farrall, S., Short, E., Cowan, L. and Gruer, L., "Alcohol, drug use and sexual behaviour of young adults on a Mediterranean holiday", *Addiction Research*, 1998, 6 (4): 319–340; and in Khan, F., Ditton, J., Elliott, L., Short, E., Morrison, A., Farrall, S. and Gruer, L. "EscapeEs: How the ecstasy using holidaymaker eludes post-modern theory" in S. Carter and S. Clift (eds) *Tourism and Sex: Culture, Commerce and Coercion*, Cassell, London, 2000.

3   Howe, R., Pattenden, S., Mill, A. and Edwards, J. "Mixmag drug survey", *Mixmag*, 105, February 2000: 62–79.

Acknowledgements

This book uses data from two studies of Ecstasy use undertaken in Glasgow in the 1990s. Alasdair Forsyth and Sally Haw were responsible for setting up the main study, and for recruiting the first part of the large sample. Emma Short took over from them, completed the recruitment and, with Samuel Phillips, began the quantitative work. Richard Hammersley and Jason Ditton completed the detailed quantitative analysis, and Furzana Khan conducted the qualitative interviews. Iain Smith, Asim Suddle and Dominic Gallagher provided the necessary professional psychiatric input, and Gail Cooper, Karen Scott, Desiree Allen and John Oliver the professional forensic advice. Lesley Henderson helped with the study of the information needs of Ecstasy users, reported in the Appendix.

We are indebted to the Chief Scientist at the Scottish Office for providing the funds necessary to collect the data reported in the five main chapters, and to the Health Education Board for Scotland for funding the research reported in the Appendix. The views expressed here do not necessarily represent the views of either body.

Drug users know more about drugs than do drug experts. Without the assistance of our respondents, none of this would have been possible.

CHAPTER ONE
Introduction – Getting into Ecstasy

In many ways, Ecstasy is an extraordinary drug. What particularly distinguishes it from everything that came before was the deliberate choice of such an advertiser's dream of a name for the rather less easily pronounceable MDMA (or, to be even more technical, 3-4-methylenedioxymethamphetamine). Rumour even has it that "empathy" was field tested as a candidate name, but that "Ecstasy" had more sales appeal. Furthermore, its apparently curious affect – a mixture of the energetic effects of, say, amphetamines, and the psychedelic effects of, for example, LSD – even meant that a whole new substance class, "entactogens", had to be coined for experts to find somewhere to place it.

Although it only burst on the British scene in a big way in the early 1990s,[4] drifting over, it seems, from the raver's holiday paradise island of Ibiza, it was first patented by the German pharmaceutical giant, Merck, in 1912. Actually, the original patent had been issued on Christmas Eve of that year, and perhaps this is why one of its nicknames is "eve". Apart from the almost obligatory appearance in the notorious American army drug trials of the 1950s, little was heard of it thereafter until it surfaced as the psychotherapists" drug of choice in California in the late 1960s. They referred to it, incidentally, by another nickname: "adam".

The American Drug Enforcement Agency succeeded in having it criminalised in 1985, and in the most restrictive category of all. In Britain, too, it is similarly heavily penalised: here as a Class A Dangerous Drug. It could be said that this has not really had the desired effect. Estimates of the extent of use range from 200,000 to

5 million uses per week in Britain, although 1 million weekly uses is a widely accepted benchmark. The media (as we shall see in Chapter Five) paint only a dreary picture of Ecstasy-death on first consumption of an Ecstasy tablet – something which, given even the lowest estimate of the frequency of weekly use, must be a highly unusual event.

What would be a more typical experience of using Ecstasy for the first time? We start with a few experiences from our research subjects, before describing them, and how we recruited them. As we will see, right from the start people report very different experiences on this drug.

"It was magic. All your muscles relax, and you felt this great surge of energy..." (Phil)

"One of the best nights of my life, and I've been sort of hooked on the feeling ever since. I had an amazing night!...the next thing I knew, I was in the middle of the dance floor...in the middle of the dance floor on my own...I just had this uncontrollable urge to dance, and I just spent the rest of the night going "Give me more! Give me more!'..." (Gael)

"I didn't really know exactly how it was supposed to make you feel. I knew it was supposed to make you feel happy, but that's the only thing I knew about it. I never asked. I just took it, and that was that...It didn't make me communicative: I think the opposite. I just felt that I've got thoughts, but I don't want to speak. I was just happy not talking at all...Ecstasy makes you sort of sit there with a big smile on your face, not talking..." (Sandra)

"The first time I ever took it...it didn't work. It was about the 4th or 5th one that I took before it...but to start with, I only took a wee bit. I never took a whole one for a while..." (Agnes)

Who are these people? How did we get them to talk to us?

GETTING THE LARGE SAMPLE TO COMPLETE QUESTIONNAIRES

Finding Ecstasy Users

This book is based mainly on two sources of information. First, we interviewed 229 Glaswegians using a detailed questionnaire. Of this group, which we call the "large sample", 20 had never used Ecstasy, 8 had quit using Ecstasy, and 201 were still using it. Second, we tape-recorded in-depth qualitative interviews with 22 of these Ecstasy users, and material from these interviews is referred to as coming from the "small group". Just before we completed the book, we re-interviewed 7 of the 22 again.

People were recruited for the large sample using a now conventional community "snowballing" strategy. Ecstasy users were contacted – the initial criterion for inclusion in the study was that people had taken Ecstasy at least once – in a variety of ways and in a variety of settings. If convinced of our good intentions, and if they knew other Ecstasy users, these initial interviewees often themselves gave us the names and addresses of other people for us to interview.

The emerging demographic profile of the growing sample was monitored regularly, and with greater and greater stringency as the sample grew in size. Starting in December, 1993, everyone available was interviewed in the early stages, beginning with 8 "first contacts" to different potential chains. However, it soon became apparent that – perhaps given the prevalence of Ecstasy use – chains seemed inexhaustible, and that interviews were mostly with experienced poly-drug users in their mid-twenties that, as a group, had a rather middle class skew. These were practically all Ecstasy users, some of them heavy users, but it appeared that they had merely added Ecstasy to the other drugs that they used from time to time.

This is not altogether unusual, as the idealised research search for one-drug users always has to contend with an untidier reality choice between non-drug and poly-drug use. However, a small group of relatively ubiquitous drugs (cannabis, amphetamines, nitrites, LSD and Ecstasy) is believed to be the drug group of choice of those dancing for many hours at "raves".[5] Those in this sample who conformed to this use pattern were termed "predominant Ecstasy users", although it is recognised that their cannabis (and possibly amphetamine and LSD) use might be more frequent. By the end of March 1994 (and with the completion of 76 interviews), only 37% of the sample could be classified as "predominant Ecstasy users". (The search for "only Ecstasy users" failed to find a single interviewee).

Accordingly, the recruitment strategy was reviewed at the end of March 1994 (after the first four months' fieldwork). There are no formal scientific techniques for this, because "snowballing" operates in an environment where the nature, type and size of the population being sampled is itself unknown. Jerome Beck and Marsha Rosenbaum in their excellent American study of Ecstasy use,[6] faced the same problem in collecting their sample of 100 Ecstasy users, and commented on page 164 of their book:

"We made decisions as to whether a particular chain had been exhausted and when and where a new chain should be started using "theoretical sampling". When we felt that a particular population (such as Jewish professionals, "New Age Seekers") had been saturated, we would stop interviewing its members. On the other hand, when we learned through interviews of previously unknown groups who were using MDMA (such as "postpunk New Wavers"), we attempted to procure subjects from that group."

By the tenth month of fieldwork, continual monitoring indicated that we were unsuccessful at recruiting Ecstasy users in employment. Subsequently, interviews for the remainder of the fieldwork period were restricted to those in work. This reflexive procedure proved very successful, and interviewing concluded on the 9th June, 1995.

The questionnaire used was unusual in the sense that although it asked the normal questions about the frequency of use of various illegal and legal drugs, it also asked a great many apparently irrelevant "lifestyle" questions. The reason was this: typically drug researchers just ask about drugs users about their drug use. The only picture that they can thereafter paint of them is as "drug users" – first, last and always, and as if they did nothing else, and were not, as we were to find out, just as "normal", in practically all respects, as the rest of us. We followed the main questionnaire by administering various well-known psychiatric scales, to test the idea – believed by many – that Ecstasy use leads to depression. In short, we found no evidence of this.[7]

We also harvested a small sample of head hair from all those willing to donate it, to test the idea that traces of Ecstasy use can be discovered in metabolitic form in hair. The laboratories we used found very little relationship between amount of Ecstasy use that our respondents claimed to have indulged in, and the metabolitic evidence found in their hair. We don't know whether this was because of memory failure and/or consumption of adulterated tablets masquerading as Ecstasy, or because of laboratory error (although we have no reason to suspect the latter).[8]

What was the Ecstasy Using Sample Like?

The 229-strong large sample was composed of 101 women (44%) and 128 men (56%). Ages ranged from 14 to 44 (average age was 23), with 46 (20%) being 19 years old or younger, 112 (49%) between 20 and 24 years old, and the remaining 71 (31%) being 25 years old or older. The males were slightly older than the females (typical age of males was 21, that of females was 20). Of the total, 221 (97%) described themselves as white.

The target for the sample was "Glaswegians", and the achieved distribution reflects actual general population distribution of the city reasonably (47, 21% from the city centre; 63, 28% from the West end; 58, 25% from the rest of the city; 36, 16% from the suburbs; and 24, 11% from the immediately surrounding countryside). We don't mean to imply by this that our sample is necessarily representative of the city: just that we succeeded in recruiting people from, literally, all "walks" of life in and around Glasgow. Males were more likely to reside in the West end and in the rest of the city, and females more likely to come from the suburbs and from the surrounding countryside. Younger people were far more likely to live in the suburbs, and much more likely to live with their parents, although young women were no more likely to do this than were young men.

Most (191, 83%) were single, with only 7 (3%) being married, and 28 (12%) cohabiting. The sample only had 19 children between them, and these were no more likely to belong to the married or cohabiting members than to the single ones. A large number lived alone (103, 45%), a further 61 (27%) lived with their parents (particularly, the younger members of the sample), with the remaining 65 (28%) living with partners or friends. Males were slightly more likely to live on their own, and females slightly more likely to live with their parents. Only about a third (80, 35%) lived in owned accommodation, with the remainder being in either state or private rental sector. Those living with their parents were only slightly more likely to be in owned accommodation than were those who lived alone or with others.

Education levels attained were rather higher than those typical for most groups of researched drug users and more similar to the cocaine users we studied before we began to research Ecstasy use.[9] Thirteen (6%) had no qualifications, 46 (20%) only O levels, 72 (31%) had A levels or equivalent, 42 (18%) a college qualification, 45 (20%) a university degree, and, finally, 11 (5%) a postgraduate degree. There was no gender difference, but an obvious age one. Although more educated than many other drug user samples, this sample was not as educated as the 100 Ecstasy users studied by Beck & Rosenbaum, of whom, 72% had a university degree.

About a third (79, 35%) were working when interviewed, with another third (73, 32%) being on unemployment benefit, 52 (23%) being students, and the remainder (25, 11%) being either sick, homebound or on an employment training scheme. Men were much more likely to be in receipt of unemployment benefit, and women were slightly more likely to be in work, or studying. Those in receipt of unemployment benefit were also more likely to claim an illegal income. Class is always difficult to establish. Here, each respondent was asked for both his father's and mother's occupation, and the typical paternal occupation was B; for maternal occupation, C1. Respondents reporting fathers in low status occupations tended to report mothers in the same or slightly higher status occupations. Those reporting fathers in high status occupations tended to report mothers in the slightly lower or markedly lower status occupations.

Respondents were asked to detail their weekly income, divided into their total illegal income and their total legal income. Most people (158, 71%) claimed to have no illegal income (and 5 no legal income). Most of the 66 (29%) with an illegal income made less than £50 a week this way, and most of these only had a small legal income. The few with the larger illegal incomes tended to have large legal incomes. Males were more likely to be the bigger earners in total, and this was also true for illegal income. Older people had bigger legal incomes, naturally enough, although this was not true for illegal income, where those aged 20-24 were more likely to be the big earners than those aged 25 and over.[10]

When the non-users were compared to the Ecstasy users, the former were slightly more likely to be female, were roughly the same age, had similar marital status, were no more or less likely to have children, were drawn from the same locations, and had similar living arrangements. The non-users were considerably better educated, although were no more likely to be in work or in receipt of unemployment benefit, and their incomes were broadly similar.

All respondents who had ever taken Ecstasy answered an array of questions about their lifetime use of Ecstasy, and a very extensive set of questions relating to their use of Ecstasy in the 12 months prior to interview. These included estimations of the number of days on which they had consumed Ecstasy for each of the previous 12 months, together with an estimation of how many Ecstasy tablets they had taken on each day of use.

Their Use of Ecstasy

We then used this information to classify our users in terms of their tablet consumption in the past 12 months. The result is in Table 1.1.[11] Eight users had not used in the past year, and so are grouped with the 20 non users. The "Light" users had consumed between 1 and 11 tablets in the previous year (broadly speaking, their averaged consumption was "less than monthly"); the "Medium" users had consumed between 12 and 47 tablets in the previous year (similarly, their averaged consumption was "more than monthly but less than weekly"); the "Heavy" users had consumed 48 or more tablets in the previous year (their averaged consumption was "more than weekly but less than daily").

As one would expect, older people were more likely to have used more Ecstasy, but this was not as marked as it could have been. Even though the trend was for older age groups to have used more Ecstasy, nevertheless substantial numbers even of the youngest group had used Ecstasy extensively, and many of the oldest category were members of the lowest Ecstasy using group. The lack of a strong correlation between Ecstasy use and age is, from a perspective of drug use research in general, rather more remarkable than the slight relationship found. However, this may be because Ecstasy is believed to have appeared suddenly, and in large quantities, in the late 1980s, having previously been scarce. This would

ECSTASY USING GROUPS AND DEMOGRAPHIC FACTORS

	Non-users & ex-users	Light	Medium	Heavy	ALL
n =	28	83	73	45	229
Ecstasy tablet use last year	none	<11	12–47	48>	
% female	57	43	44	38	44
% aged 14–19	18	18	21	24	20
% aged 20–24	46	47	51	51	49
% aged 25+	36	35	29	24	31
% single	71	87	91	80	83
% urban dwellers	70	81	77	58	74
% suburban dwellers	22	12	16	18	16
% country dwellers	7	7	7	24	11
% no more than O Levels	14	23	29	33	26
% A Levels/college	39	50	48	58	50
% University educated	46	27	23	9	25
% in employment	25	28	40	44	35
% unemployed	50	40	45	40	43
% student	25	33	15	16	23
% with some illegal income	32	21	30	39	29
% with £91+ weekly illegal income	7	1	8	17	7
% with £91+ weekly total income	32	44	52	64	49

Key: n = shows number of respondents, < means "less than", > means "greater than", % is percentage.

Table 1.1

have restricted the opportunity for older people to have used it for longer, and thus to have consumed more.

There was no great relationship between gender and Ecstasy using group (although males were more likely to be heavy users, they were also more likely to be light users), nor between different user groups and domiciliary residence in or around Glasgow, or marital status, but there was one between attained education and Ecstasy use.

Compared to the others, some heavy users were most likely to be unqualified, but others were, conversely, those most likely to have a postgraduate degree. The typical level of attainment for each group was Highers/A Levels. There are differences, but not in any obvious or straightforward direction. Non-users were most likely to have a university degree of some or other sort, and light use was not associated with high educational achievement, and heavy use not with low educational achievement. Age, inevitably, explains more of the educational data than does Ecstasy consumption.

The whole sample, and each user group taken separately, had more members who lived on their own than lived in any other single way. There is no other obvious patterning (and there was no association between type of housing tenure and user group, or in parental occupation – whether paternal or maternal – and user group).

Non-users and light users were most likely to be students, the medium users more likely than other Ecstasy users to be in work, and the heavy users most likely to be unemployed. This pattern was broadly matched by patterns of total income, except that here, large numbers of heavy users were higher earners. The heavy users were more likely than any other user group to have had a medium or high illegal income (10 of them did, compared to only 6 from all the other groups, and 7 of these were officially unemployed).

THE SMALL GROUP THAT TALKED TO US ON TAPE

Well, the book is mostly about them, so we should describe all 22 by way of introduction. We followed them up so that we could put some animated conversational flesh on the otherwise rather dry bones of the quantitative data. We start with "Charlie" (all names have been changed, as has any other information which might permit anybody to be identified), our ex-user:

"Charlie" was 22, unemployed, and cohabiting in the southern part of the city with his partner. He had no paper qualifications, and his last job was working in a bar. Still, he swam more than once a week, and was a weekly hill walker and runner. He believed in God, worshiped regularly (a Buddhist), but thought he wouldn't vote if there were a general election tomorrow. He first tried Ecstasy in America 8 years before we first interviewed him, and had taken it over 100 times since (once taking 48 tablets in a 4 day binge) but not at all in the previous year. He was a daily tobacco smoker, but took no other (legal or illegal) substance. He has had sex on Ecstasy, but that was several years previously. He evaded paying fares on public transport now and again, and bought stolen goods occasionally. When we first interviewed him, he said that he no longer suffered from insomnia and blackouts, but still had memory problems, concentration problems, depression, paranoia and mood swings. He had been receiving psychiatric assistance for these disorders.

Next come the light users of Ecstasy. We present their potted biographies in order of ascending age. First, "Tam":

"Tam" was 16 when we interviewed him first, and was still at school doing his highers after getting 7 O grades. He lived with his parents in a relatively run-down area of inner-city Glasgow. He was a keen footballer (and spectator, particularly of Celtic), and read the *Sun* and the *News of the World*. Although without any political views, he believed in God. He had first taken Ecstasy a year earlier, with friends at a party, and had only taken it about 6 times since. He actually didn't think much of it, and only took it at clubs where he felt that he needed it to enjoy himself. He didn't smoke tobacco (except with cannabis), and in the last year had only taken amphetamines and LSD as well as Ecstasy. Although only arrested once, he claimed to have travelled on public transport for free, driven a car without a licence, stolen money, damaged property, shoplifted, carried a weapon, bought stolen goods, and been in a fight – all in the last year. He suffered occasionally from mood swings, but didn't know whether or not this was because of the drugs he used. "*Ecstasy*", he thought, "*makes you go stupid*" and "*rots your brain cells*".

"Sharon" was 19, worked in the beauty industry and lived with her parents out of town. She left school with a handy clutch of O grades, and gained a City & Guilds qualification thereafter. To keep fit, she did step-aerobics on a daily basis, stayed in most nights, and never read a newspaper. Not having a car, she spent a lot of money on clothes. Politically, she saw herself as in the centre, but thought she would vote for the SNP if there were a general election tomorrow. She had taken Ecstasy for the first time (in a club with friends, all of whom had taken it before) a year before we first interviewed her, and had had it 8 times since then. She was a daily tobacco user, and a weekly alcohol and cannabis user. She, too, took amphetamines about once a fortnight, and cocaine and poppers less frequently. Once, in the past year, she took LSD. The only time she had had sex the previous year, she was on Ecstasy. She had bought things known to be stolen during the previous year, suffered from memory problems, insomnia, paranoia and mood swings, but didn't know why.

"**Kirsty**" was a single, 21 year old student who shared a flat with friends in Glasgow's west end. Successful at school, she was studying for a university degree. She was a keen hill walker and *Guardian* reader, SNP inclined but doubtful that she would bother to vote if an election were called tomorrow. She first took Ecstasy in a night club when out with friends. That was 2 years before we first interviewed her, and she had only taken it again 11 times since. She had never binged, or thought of giving it up, but did once go 4 months without using it. She was an almost daily tobacco smoker, a twice weekly cannabis user, and a once weekly alcohol drinker. Apart from the odd line of cocaine or amphetamine, and the occasional LSD tab, Kirsty took few other drugs. She had had a couple of male sexual partners in the past year, but didn't try sex and Ecstasy with either of them. Aside from occasional public transport fare evasion, she couldn't recall committing any other crime. She suffered from memory and concentrations problems, but didn't know why either.

"**Gael**" worked in the media, and was a single 20 year old living with her parents east of the city. She did well at school, and gained vocational/technical qualifications thereafter. She swam once a week, but never read a newspaper. Gael didn't believe in God, but believed in the SNP and would vote for them if an election were held tomorrow. She first took Ecstasy at a rave 4 years ago, and had taken it about 15 times since. When we first interviewed her, she was a light Ecstasy user, who had never binged, nor thought about giving up (although she once went 5 months without taking any). She didn't earn much, but because her parents didn't charge her rent, she spent a large part of her income on legal and illegal drugs. She drank alcohol most days of the week, and was a daily tobacco and cannabis user. Apart from that, only the occasional valium and line of amphetamine. Without a steady partner at that time, she had had a couple of casual sexual experiences in the past year, but neither of them was combined with taking Ecstasy. She still occasionally shoplifted and sold drugs, and suffered from memory problems, depression and mood swings for no – as far as she could see – apparent reason.

"**Danny**" earned a good salary by following his father's footsteps into the chemical industry. Although he left school without any Higher grade exams, he got a relevant HND afterwards. Aged 21 when we first interviewed him, he still lived with his parents, played rugby weekly, and worked out in a gym more often. A Christian, he would vote conservative if there were an election tomorrow. He read the *Daily Telegraph* once a week, and the *Daily Record* and *Evening Times* more often. He first took Ecstasy 4 years prior to first interview (at a club, with friends) because he was told it was "cleaner" than taking amphetamines. He had taken Ecstasy about 60 times since then, but in the last year he had reduced use to becoming merely a light user, although he used it when having sex with 3 of the 4 sexual partners he had the previous year. He had never binged on it, and indeed, gave up entirely once for 5 months. He was a daily tobacco smoker, a twice weekly alcohol drinker, and a frequent cannabis user. Apart from that, just the occasional LSD tab. In the last year, he had been in the odd fight, and had bought stolen goods now and again. He had had occasional memory problems and suffered now and again from insomnia, but didn't know why.

"**Naomi**" was a 23 year old single woman who rented a flat with friends in the rather smart West end area of Glasgow to which she had moved from central Scotland about 7 years previously. She had a degree, but could only find work as a sales assistant when we first interviewed her. Another *Guardian* reader, she walked daily, and both went to aerobics and cycled at least once a week. She was a committed Christian and a labour voter. She first took Ecstasy, out of curiosity, with friends at a club about 6 years ago before we first interviewed her, and thought she had taken it about 30 times since. When we interviewed her, she was a light user, who had never binged, but who once gave up Ecstasy for 2 months after a tablet made her feel ill, and only tried sex and Ecstasy together once. Apart from alcohol (2 days out of 3), she used both cannabis and cocaine about once a month. Her only other criminal activity in the last year had been to fiddle an insurance claim. She didn't suffer from any medical problems, but thought Ecstasy could make you feel paranoid.

"**Euan**" was a 27 year old single man working in the media and living on the south side of the city. Success at school followed by gaining a university degree had given him the sort of income that allowed him to run a car. He played rugby once a week, and football twice. Because of his job, he read as many newspapers and magazines as he could (but he didn't have to pay for them). He believed in neither God nor voting. He was given his first Ecstasy in a night club when out with friends 4 years before we first interviewed him, and had used it about 12 times since. He was a light user, who had never binged, and once had gone 18 months without using Ecstasy. He drank alcohol every day, tobacco very occasionally, and cannabis hardly at all. A bit of amphetamine and cocaine, and that was it for Euan. He had a steady partner, and they had tried sex on Ecstasy. Apart from a few youthful indiscretions, he had done nothing else criminal in the year prior to interview. Apart from occasional insomnia, he suffered no regular medical problems.

"**Stuart**" was a 28-year old student, who lived with his parents as he had always done, in a rather smart residential area near central Glasgow. He didn't get very good school qualifications, but was then studying for an HND. He was self-employed in the service sector, and bought and sold stolen goods to make some extra cash. He was very keen on fitness, and practised martial arts and weightlifting several times a week. He believed in God, but was inclined to Buddhism and spiritualism. He was concerned about "green" issues, but reckoned he would vote SNP if there was an election tomorrow. He first took Ecstasy 4 years ago (he bought one at a night club because he was curious) but had only taken 8 tablets since. Once he tried having sex on Ecstasy, but had been drinking alcohol at the same time, and couldn't remember much about it. However, he was a daily tobacco and cannabis smoker, very occasionally taking heroin and cocaine (although he had never injected anything) and now and again used amphetamines, LSD and poppers. He had had quite a few medical problems in the previous year, and thought these (which included memory problems, insomnia, concentration problems, paranoia and mood swings) might have been related to his drug use.

"**Richie**", 30 when we first interviewed him, came from a poor background, but did well at school, went on to university to get a degree, and worked in higher education. He shared a flat with friends, and had done so since he moved to Glasgow several years ago. Another sportsman (swimming, running and football), he was a daily *Guardian* reader, an occasional *Evening Times* one, and a weekly *Big Issue* purchaser. A left-winger and intending labour voter, he was also an atheist. He first took Ecstasy with friends at a club 4 years previously, and had taken it about 25 times since. When we interviewed him, he was a light user, bingeing only once (with four or five tablets consumed over 2 days), and had never tried having sex on Ecstasy. He was a heavy alcohol and tobacco user, adding cannabis a couple of days a week , amphetamines about once a fortnight, with the occasional line of cocaine, and tab of LSD. Although not having an entirely crime-free past, in the previous year he had only got involved in a fight once, and sold drugs on a few occasions. He suffered occasionally from blackouts, but if this was drug-related, then it probably stemmed from the alcohol rather than anything else.

"**Fraser**", at 43, was older than most of the Ecstasy users, and lived with his wife and two children. He left school with few qualifications, but had since studied for and obtained a diploma that led him on to work in education. He claimed to "get by" on his smallish salary, and although he owned a car, was a keen walker. He was a *Guardian* reader but didn't read it every day. As left-wing as any of those interviewed, he didn't believe in God, but was inclined towards Buddhism. He first took Ecstasy at home with his wife, and in the five years since before being first interviewed by us, had taken it about 150 times. He and his wife have tried having sex on Ecstasy, but only once. In the previous year, he had become a light user. He was a daily cannabis (and tobacco) user, but apart from that, only did cocaine, amphetamines, mushrooms, LSD and Ecstasy a few times a year. He did a bit of shoplifting and so on in the past, but in the last year had only bought a few stolen goods and sold drugs. He also had had an alcohol problem in the past, and was still attending AA meetings.

Next, the medium level users. "Liz" first:

"**Liz**" was a 19-year old who worked in information services, who shared a flat with friends in Glasgow's west end. Leaving school with good qualifications, she got the job and career she had always wanted. She exercised a lot (aerobics, gymnastics, swimming and walking), and was another *Guardian* reader. She was a non-practising Christian who would vote labour if an election were held tomorrow. She had taken her first Ecstasy at a club a year before we first interviewed her, and had taken it about 20 times since. She had never binged, nor thought of giving it up, although she thought she might do so in the future. She was also a heavy alcohol drinker and cannabis smoker (taking both more than five days a week), occasionally took amphetamines and cocaine – and, even less frequently, mushrooms and LSD. She had a steady partner, and they had tried having sex on Ecstasy in the past year. She confessed to no other criminal activity ever, and had no medical problems apart from occasional lapses of concentration.

"Iain" was a single 20-year old textile worker who lived with one of his parents and one other sibling in a local town known for its textile industry. He didn't exercise, but he read the *Sun*, and owned a car. He didn't believe in God, and wouldn't vote. Like many, he had had his first Ecstasy when in a club with friends 5 years ago, and had taken Ecstasy about 30 times since then. When we first interviewed him, he was a medium level user, who had binged quite heavily on occasion. He hardly ever drank alcohol, but smoked tobacco daily, and cannabis every other day. In the previous year, apart from taking Ecstasy about 15 times, he had occasionally taken amphetamines, LSD and poppers. He had never tried sex on Ecstasy, and claimed to suffer no medical problems.

"Agnes" was a 20 year old in the beauty industry who lived out of the city with her parents and two sisters. Leaving school at 15 with 2 O grades, she later got a SCOTVEC qualification. She did aerobics, but only once a week. She read the *Evening Times* daily, but most of her spare money went on running her car, and buying clothes. She was a weak labour supporter, but thought she wouldn't bother to vote if a general election were held tomorrow. Her first Ecstasy? Like many, in a night club with friends, and out of curiosity. That was 2 years before we first interviewed her, and she calculated then that she had taken Ecstasy 36 times since, making her medium level user when we first interviewed her. She had a steady partner then, but had had sex on Ecstasy with one casual partner the previous year. She smoked cannabis a couple of times a week, but tobacco and alcohol only once. These aside, she took amphetamines about once a fortnight. She has never done anything else illegal (apart from driving a car without a licence, once), but suffers from memory problems and paranoia sometimes, for reasons which then escaped her.

"**Morag**" was in the beauty industry, was 22 years old, single, and lived on her own, but outside the city. With only 4 O grades, she gained a vocational qualification after leaving school. She was into step-aerobics "most days", never read a newspaper, and bought few clothes as most of her available money went to pay her mortgage. She believed in God, but not in voting (if there was an election tomorrow). She had been persuaded to try Ecstasy for the first time when at a rave with friends, most of whom had already tried it. That was 4 years before we first interviewed her, and she'd had Ecstasy about 50 times since then. Like Agnes, she had tried having sex on Ecstasy, but with her steady partner. Morag was a daily tobacco and cannabis user, but only drank alcohol once a week. Apart from that, amphetamines once a month, and cocaine twice a year. In the past (but not in the previous year) she had bought something she knew had been stolen, but apart from that her "criminality" was restricted to using illegal drugs. She occasionally suffered from paranoia, but didn't know why.

"**Sandra**" was 24 and co-habiting with her partner in a relatively cheap part of the city. She got 5 highers at school, a university degree and an information technology qualification after that. She was unemployed when we first interviewed her, but by the time we later interviewed her on tape, she had found a job in information technology. That then provided her only income. Sandra was a keen sportswoman: she swam, cycled and played badminton on a regular basis. She read the *Guardian* and the *Herald* most days, and although not a member of any political party, was an avowed left-winger. She was a vegetarian, and unsure of the existence of God. She had only been using Ecstasy for 3 years when we first interviewed her, and first bought it at a club and took it there with a friend. Since starting Ecstasy, she thought she had had about 100 tablets, but had now settled down as a medium level user, taking it about once a month. She had only tried having sex on Ecstasy once – with her steady partner during the previous year. She had never binged, but she had never given up Ecstasy either. She was a fairly heavy user of tobacco and alcohol, but wasn't a heavy user of other drugs, having only taken cannabis, amphetamines, LSD, poppers and Ecstasy a few times in the previous year. She had shoplifted (and also fiddled an insurance claim) in the past, but in the previous year the only illegal thing she had done – apart from drug use – had been to travel on public transport without paying the fare. She had never experienced any problems from her use of drugs.

Finally, the heavy Ecstasy users. We begin with "Moira":

"Moira" – 19 – had left school two years previously with 9 O grades to work in a retail fashion outlet. She lived with her parents in a local town, but was then unemployed and living on benefit. Although she didn't take any exercise, she did, at least, read the *Daily Record* every day. She was an atheistic Liberal Democrat intending voter, who had first tried Ecstasy 3 years ago at a night club, and who had taken it about 20 times since. Her parents didn't charge her for her keep, which allowed her to spend most of her money on drugs. This also permitted her to be a heavy user when we first interviewed her, and she was also a daily tobacco smoker, a weekly alcohol drinker, and a twice-weekly cannabis user. In the previous year, she had also used temazepam, valium, amphetamines (a lot) and LSD. She had had two casual sexual partners in the previous year, and had tried sex with Ecstasy with both of them. She had evaded paying fares on public transport in the previous year, bought things known to be stolen, and sold drugs other than Ecstasy. She suffered from memory and concentration problems, insomnia, depression, paranoia and mood swings, and put this down to her use of Ecstasy.

"Phil" was a 19 year old single man who lived with his parents and sisters in the southern part of the city. He got good O grades at school, but left without taking highers. With a relevant HNC qualification, he was then working as an apprentice in the engineering industry. He only read a football newspaper, and played football himself very occasionally. He spent almost as much each week paying off the loan he had taken out to buy a car as he spent on drugs. A believer in God, he had attended church recently. He viewed his politics as on the right, but claimed that he would vote labour if there were a general election tomorrow. Like many others, he had taken his first Ecstasy tablet in a club with friends. That was 2 years before we interviewed him, and he had since taken Ecstasy about 35 times, being a fairly heavy user, who had never tried combining sexual intercourse with Ecstasy. He had only binged once, and the only thing that stopped him taking more Ecstasy was lack of money. He was a daily tobacco user, but only used alcohol and cannabis about twice a week. He used LSD about once every three weeks, and poppers, mushrooms and amphetamines less frequently. In the previous year, he had driven without a licence, fiddled an insurance claim, bought stolen goods and been involved in fights, but had never even been arrested. He claimed to have had mood swings occasionally, but nothing more.

"Douglas" did well at school, but gained no vocational qualifications afterwards. Aged 20 and single when we first interviewed him, he shared a flat with friends in an inexpensive inner-city part of Glasgow, and worked in catering. His work was physical, so he didn't take any additional exercise. He never read a newspaper, and said he wouldn't bother to vote if there was a general election tomorrow. He first tried Ecstasy when out in the street with a group of friends, all of whom had already tried it. That was 3 years previously, since when he reckoned he had had about 110 Ecstasy tablets, but only once when having sex with his then regular partner. He was still a heavy user, but an erratic one. He had never binged, and only ever "thought about" giving up. He didn't drink alcohol, but was a daily smoker and near daily cannabis user. Apart from that, just the occasional line of amphetamine. He carried a weapon, and occasionally got into fights. In the previous year, he had also evaded paying the fare on public transport, and bought things known to be stolen. He had suffered unintentional weight loss, memory problems, insomnia, concentration problems, paranoia and mood swings – all of which he attributed to his drug use.

"Willie" was a 24-year old then unemployed man who lived with his partner and one child in a relatively inexpensive part of inner-city Glasgow. He got several O grades and a couple of highers at school, and later picked up a vocational qualification from a local college. His was on benefits, but regularly made a couple of hundred pounds a week working on the side (mostly dealing drugs other than Ecstasy). He was a heavy clubber, a vegan, an occasional cyclist and *Sun* reader, and a believer in God (but not in any political party). He got his first Ecstasy from a dealer, and tried it at a friend's house. In the 6 years since he started, he reckoned that he had taken over 200 Ecstasy tablets. His use of it over the previous year was both heavy and erratic, but he had only had sexual intercourse when using it on a couple of occasions. He used to binge on Ecstasy, but also had occasionally given it up altogether (for as long as a year, once). In the previous year, he had used most drugs available (cannabis daily, alcohol a couple of days a week, temazepam, cocaine and heroin weekly, but not tobacco, temgesic, solvents, mushrooms or ketamine) although he had never injected anything, nor binged on Ecstasy. In the past year, he had done a bit of shoplifting, bought stolen goods, and used public transport without paying the fare. He claimed to have had both memory problems and blackouts from using drugs.

"Kath" was a 25-year old woman who worked in the media and lived with friends in a flat located outside the city. She had a postgraduate degree, and her income allowed her to run a car. Because of her job, perhaps, she was a daily reader of the *Guardian*, the *Independent* and the *Scotsman*, and a weekly aerobics practitioner. Politically, she was far left, and would vote labour. She first took Ecstasy 5 years before we first spoke to her, at a private party where most of the other guests had taken it before. She was a heavy Ecstasy user when we interviewed her, and reckoned she had taken about 175 tablets since first trying it. She had had 4 sexual partners in the past year, and tried Ecstasy simultaneously with sex with only one of them. She sold Ecstasy quite frequently, but that was her only illegal pastime. She had only binged once, and said that she could not remember a time when she was "off" Ecstasy. She was a daily tobacco smoker, a weekly alcohol drinker (and weekly Ecstasy user) and a monthly cannabis user. She had had cocaine a couple of times the previous year, and amphetamines about once a fortnight. She thought that her occasional attacks of paranoia, and more regular mood swings were a result of her drug use.

"Fiona" was a 27-year old public sector worker, who lived with her husband in their own house. She did reasonably well at school and acquired a relevant HND qualification after leaving. She wasn't a big earner, didn't exercise at all, and read the *Herald* on most days. She believed in God, and, if an election were held tomorrow, the Liberal Democrat party would get her vote. She took her first Ecstasy at a private party 6 years before being first interviewed, and calculated that she had taken it over 300 times since then. She was currently a heavy Ecstasy user, regularly taking 8 tablets a month, and spending over £30 a week on it. She also smoked tobacco daily, and cannabis three times a week. Apart from that (and an occasional line of cocaine or amphetamine) nothing. She had tried Ecstasy when having sex with her husband, and more generally attributed her insomnia, paranoia and mood swings to her Ecstasy use.

Overall, 22 very ordinary people from varied backgrounds, with varied careers and interests, who use various substances and sometimes do some other things that are against the law. It is worth remembering that about a third of Scottish men enter their thirties having received a criminal conviction of some kind, so one cannot jump to conclusions about drug use and crime in this group.

HOW THEY GOT INTO ECSTASY

Most of our data here comes from asking the large sample a series of simple questions about their first use of Ecstasy such as: when you first took Ecstasy, where were you? Who were you with? How did you get it? If bought, who did you buy it from? Why did you take it? Was it what you expected? Had you been offered it before? And, if offered before, why didn't you take it then? In the more open conversations with the small group, the issue surfaced now and again, and they were particularly forthcoming about why they first took Ecstasy, and what the experience was like.

Those in the large sample were far more likely to have taken their first Ecstasy tablet at a club than anywhere else (56% did). Another 18% had started at some other dance event, leaving 26% who first tried Ecstasy in some other setting. Younger users were more likely to have taken their first Ecstasy tablet in a club, and older ones more likely to have been in some other setting such as at home, or at an illegal party. Some, as we show in research reported elsewhere,[12] even started when on holiday.

For most, first use wasn't a solitary experience: 81% said that they had taken their first Ecstasy when in a group of other people (not necessarily Ecstasy users). Most of the remainder took their first Ecstasy with one or two other people, and only 6 (3%) said that they had had their first Ecstasy experience alone.

Overall, nearly a quarter (25%) got their first Ecstasy tablet free, 58% asked for and paid for it, while only 17% were offered a tablet, without soliciting it, for which they then paid. Younger initiates were more likely than older ones to have got their first tablet for nothing. This was also true for women.

Half got their first tablet from a dealer, the other half from a user. Age doesn't come into it, but women were much more likely to get their first Ecstasy from a user than were males (who were correspondingly more likely to get theirs from a dealer). However, "dealer" doesn't necessarily mean "stranger". Only 14% got their Ecstasy from a stranger. These were mostly previously unknown dealers. Only 3 new users obtained their first Ecstasy from another user they were not acquainted with. Of the rest, 42% got their first Ecstasy from a dealer (one they knew well, or were friends or acquaintances with), and 35% from a user who was a friend or an acquaintance.

Why Did They Take It?

Why did they take it? About 40% just stated, "curiosity", with the 31% who said that they "wanted to try it" presumably meaning much the same thing. Of the rest, 9% had "heard it was good", 7% thought it was the "right occasion", with the remaining 13% giving some other reason. Some members of the small group offered other reasons.

Recommendations of friends, coupled to curiosity, were the most frequently cited reasons for getting into Ecstasy. The amount that these interviewees knew about Ecstasy before taking it varied from the memory of Sandra (an employed 24 year old who was a medium level user):

"Nothing, absolutely nothing. I didn't really know exactly how it was supposed to make you feel. I knew it was supposed to make you feel happy, but that's the only thing I knew about it. I never asked. I just took it, and that was that..."

Through this from Phil (a 19 year old employed heavy user):

"My pal told me what it felt like...he said "it will make you feel good." Some made him feel dead energetic and some made him feel dead good inside, and made your stomach muscles relax, and you sat and chilled out..."

To Morag (a 22 year old employed medium level user):

"People had told me, you know, what their experience of it was...in terms of the physical and mental effects. I mean, I knew how much it cost and it was illegal, and I suppose what put me off was I was partly scared of taking it...because of stories I'd heard about people massively dehydrating and things like that, and not enjoying it, or being allergic to it in some way... That was the media, yeah, but I'd heard more people that I know having bad experiences on acid than on Ecstasy, so this was media hype, I suppose, in a way..."

And finally to Agnes (a 20 year old employed medium level user) who recalled:

"They just said it was good, and they also said that they had this once a month rule, that they only went and did it once a month, and I used to as well at the beginning. I waited for, after the first time, I waited a

month, and then after the second time I thought, "Sod it! This feels good! I'm just going to do it whenever'... you know? After then, it was every two weeks..."

For a few, however, Ecstasy offered an alternative to other drugs. As Phil (a 19 year old employed heavy user) remembered:

"I was fed up with speed, and I was totally fed up with drink. With drink, I just...I felt I only wanted to fight, and I made an idiot of myself and with speed, it just gave me a funny feeling, and so did acid. Acid kind of confused me, and confused my brain. I don't know why: I just didn't like it..."

And Danny (a 21 year old employed light user) recalled:

"There was no reason, really. I just, just decided to for a change. I'd been sick of the gouch[13] off the speed. And basically [the first time] what I bought was half an E, which cost the same as a gram of speed..."

Actually, just over half of the large sample (108, or 54%) had been offered Ecstasy before, but had not taken it. Several reasons were offered. Nearly 22% said that they had been too "scared" to try Ecstasy previously, and a further 20% that, previously, they had not been sufficiently "interested" to do so. About 16% said that they hadn't been able to afford it then, and another 16% said that the circumstances were just "wrong". The remainder gave a variety of other reasons.

What was it like?

Yet, they all did try Ecstasy at some time or other. Was it what they expected? About a third of the large sample (29%) said that it was "worse" than they had expected, with the rest saying that it was either the "same" (17%) or "better" (54%). Overall, of those 55 who said that their first experience of Ecstasy was "worse" than expected, no consistent reasons were advanced. Twenty five different reasons were advanced: with the most common reason (although only given by 5 respondents) was that they were on other drugs at the time (and presumably couldn't differentiate or appreciate the effects of the Ecstasy). The remaining reasons are a curious bunch, with some respondents saying that their first Ecstasy was "less speedy", and others that it was "just like speed". Still others claimed that it made them unable to sleep, with others saying that it made them sleepy! Other complaints related to possible adulteration, or to failure to take enough (from those who had only taken a half tablet to start with). Overall, it isn't particularly surprising that those with initial relatively negative experiences persevered. The heroin literature abounds with stories of addicted users vomiting, collapsing and so on in the early stages of use, and only becoming dependent after persisting with use and becoming physically, or failing that psychologically, tolerant of such adverse effects.

Those who said that their first Ecstasy experience was "better" than expected, again reported a wide range of reasons. Often these were just positive versions of the negatives that those who said their first experience was "worse" than expected. For example, some of those who said it was "better" claimed it was because it was "stronger", "less trippy", "better than any other". Again, there were almost as many reasons as respondents. Here, again, members of the small group give something of the range of experiences recalled from their first time.

For them, first experiences were also mixed, ranging from the highly enjoyable, through the lack of any perceived effect, to the occasional unpleasant experience. Gael (a 20 year old employed light user) claimed, for example, that the first experience was, *"one of the best nights of my life, and I've been sort of hooked on the feeling ever since. I had an amazing night!"*, and Morag (a 22 year old employed medium level user) that she immediately *"loved it, I totally loved it"*. However, Agnes remembered that *"the first time I ever took it...it didn't work. It was about the 4th or 5th one that I took before it...but to start with, I only took a wee bit. I never took a whole one for a while"*. Kirsty (a 20 year old employed medium level user) conversely took too much Ecstasy the first time she tried it, although she later became a medium level user. Here, she recalls that first evening:

"I was in a club...I took E for the first time about half way through the night. Everybody else had already took theirs. I took half. When it started coming on, I felt quite good, so I took the other half. I thought that was just it, and was going to stay that way, so I thought I would take the other half so the high would be better. But I got quite dizzy, and my sight was getting worse, kind of blurred, and the strobe light was skewing my vision, and I felt kind of faint. I fell into this guy, and he helped kind of get me to stand up, and all that. I went over to take a seat, and I felt really quite sick and dizzy, and mixed feelings really. Then it wore off, and then I got up and started dancing, and danced all night. But it was quite a

blur, that whole night. We went to a party, and my mouth kind of started going, and I couldn't really talk, like sometimes I do when I take E. I cannot talk, so I just go dead quiet...and then I start talking...just going on and gibbering really..."

More typical were recalled feelings of uncontrollable extroverted happiness, calm introverted contentment, reciprocated empathy or unbounded energy. An example of each follows. First, uncontrollable extroverted happiness, from Douglas (a 20 year old employed heavy user):

"...the most memorable feeling was more of a numbness than anything. I couldn't do anything. I don't know what I wanted to do: whether I wanted to sit down, get up, dance, walk about, go and talk to someone, or just sit in a corner by myself...I do remember that me and my friend that I halved it with standing across the dance floor from each other, standing laughing at each other in hysterics, and waving at each other, the two of us! We couldn't be bothered doing anything really, we were that mad with it the first time. But I enjoyed it. That's why I went back and tried it again..."

Second, Sandra (a 24 year old employed medium level user) remembered introverted calm contentment:

"It didn't make me communicative: I think the opposite. I just felt, that I've got thoughts, but I don't want to speak. I was just happy not talking at all. Hash makes you a lot more talkative, and speed makes you very talkative, it can make you just babble constantly, but Ecstasy makes you sort of sit there with a big smile on your face, not talking..."

Third, reciprocated empathy. Phil (a 19 year old employed heavy user):

"It was magic. All your muscles relax, and you felt this great surge of energy. It wasn't energy that you felt like jumping about...It's a kind of, don't know...when you stretch you get a kind of feeling from your body...stretching then relaxing, stretching then relaxing...a constant feeling like that. So I just sat on the couch at the back of the disco. When I first took it, me and this lassie went in [to a club] ...one of my pals bought an Eccy for him and my mate, but my mate didn't want the other half, so I took it myself, and I sat in the back, and this lassie took one as well, and it was both our first time. We just held hands.

We weren't nipping[14] or anything: we just sat in the back like that going, "This is great, isn't it?" all night. Then we tried to dance, but the feeling was just so gouchy[15] that we just couldn't dance..."

Finally, sheer energy – almost the reverse of the feeling quoted above – from Gael (a 20 year old employed light user):

"I thought, "OK, right! Sod it!" So we went up a club in town, and I took one and a half tabs...and the music was totally doing my head in before I came up on the E, because it was hard core techno...and the next thing I knew, I was in the middle of the dance floor...in the middle of the dance floor on my own...I just had this uncontrollable urge to dance, and I just spent the rest of the night going "Give me more! Give me more!' and just going about telling everyone it was my first time, and that it was totally amazing...I can remember like only being able to go downstairs for a short period of time, and then having to come back because I was rushing so much... I just felt really good. It just felt really natural. I felt like my head, my head felt straight on it, and I was having all these really nice sort of different sensations...I was with people, you know, they knew what they were doing. They knew that I was to sit down and take water, and take rests and all this..."

She continued:

"And, yeah, I just couldn't get over how at the beginning of the night I was just wandering about in this club, which was full of sort of wee neds[16], and that, you know, they looked a bit dodgy...and by the end of the night they were all, like, my best friend...I mean, honestly, it was one of the best nights of my life, but I don't have that any more when I go out and take E. I don't take Eees often, though. Well, the Eees aren't as good, and a lot of them that I've read about are not even E. I think I've just got a bit bored of it. It doesn't necessarily mean that the first time is the best time, but for me it was totally a surprise. I remember going about saying to everyone, "I didn't think I could feel this good'. That was what kept going through my head..."

Of course, these remarks all come from people who are recalling their first Ecstasy experience but who all continued to use it – with some or other degree of frequency – up until the time of the interview. We cannot tell how many first time users had negative or null initial experiences, and discontinued use thereafter.

GETTING OTHERS INTO ECSTASY

In the large sample most respondents, perhaps surprisingly given the enthusiastic way that many describe their affection for Ecstasy, were unlikely to recommend to others that they try Ecstasy. Of those still using Ecstasy, some 44% claimed never to have introduced anybody to Ecstasy, and a further 31% to have done so only to one two others. Of the remainder, only a handful (17, or 8% of the total) claimed to have introduced more than 7 people to the drug.

Persuading other People to try Ecstasy

The willingness to persuade others to try Ecstasy seems to be related to both level of use (with heavy users being more likely to), and length of using career (with those with long Ecstasy using careers being more likely to introduce others to Ecstasy, and more likely to introduce more people to it). Of those still using Ecstasy, a third (66) said that they had sold Ecstasy at least once. Of this sub-group, a quarter hadn't done it in the last year, and a further third had only done it once or twice. Inevitably, heavier users were more likely to be dealers.

In the small group, 8 (36%) said they had never introduced anybody to Ecstasy, 6 (27%) had done so to one or two others, 5 (23%) to between 3 and 7 others, and 3 (14%) to more than 7 people. Most of those who claimed never to have introduced anybody to Ecstasy had little to add when interviewed, although Iain (a 20 year old employed medium level user himself) qualified his reply in this way:

"Nil...I've never told anyone to try it. I've told them that it's good, but I've never actually taken them out and introduced them to it. Em...I was taking it before my brother, and he knew I was taking it, but I didn't actually say to him, "Go out and try it'...it was someone else that said that to him..."

And Euan (a 27 year old employed light user), who also had slight linguistic difficulty in distinguishing "recommending" from "introducing', had been careful to add safety advice to any verbal enthusiasm:

"I've said 'It's good...it's worth trying'...eh?...'Give it a go! It'll be interesting. You want to go through your life having at least tried it once....But keep yourself cool, and drink a lot of water. Keep yourself hydrated. If you're having problems, stick with the person you were talking to at the beginning, preferably with the person you're with at

the beginning of the night.'....You wouldn't tell someone to take E, and then nip off and leave them, because you want to make sure you're there for them if they have any problem with it..."

Giving simultaneous safety advice typically threaded the remarks of those that claimed to have introduced one or two others to Ecstasy, and almost all rejected the idea that they had proactively "introduced" others to it. Most claimed that they had been relatively off-hand, and balanced in their recommendations, by pointing out possible dangers as well as likely benefits. These contributions were typical:

"I told him exactly what it does. You tell them the bad with the good. You don't just tell them it's all good. It's up to them. If they're going to take it, they're going to try it anyway..."
Agnes (a 20 year old employed medium level user)

"Yeah, to a couple o' pals that havnae tried it. It's no' just been like me saying, "Take an E. Take an E. Take an E'...It's no' like, "Oh, you'd better take an E, man, "cos if you don't, you're no' goini fit in." It's more like, "Och, yeah, you should try it, it's good'. But if they don't want to try it, that's fair enough, it's entirely up to them, you know, it's not like you're goini force it..."
Moira (a 19 year old unemployed heavy user)

"I don't think...maybe...I mean, my boyfriend at the minute, he was quite wary of taking it... and when he saw that I was having a good time on it, he decided that he would try it. But I wouldn't like to think that I've ever pressurised or, em, encouraged anybody to take any- thing they didn't want to...I'll tell them what my honest opinion is, and if they decide that they want to try it, then that's up to them. But I don't think I've ever said to anybody, 'It's great! Try it!'...and I would trust that my friends are mature enough to make their own decisions..."
Liz (a 19 year old employed medium level user)

Attitudes were much the same with the group of 5 who had introduced from 3 to 7 people to Ecstasy: a mixture of safety advice, and balanced recommendation. Kath (a 25 year old employed heavy user) went to great – although not particularly successful – lengths:

"I remember once, there was this friend of mine...she's not a raver...but I had Nicholas Saunders's book, and I think...I made her read one of the essays on it, and said, 'You need to try it and see what you think, and see if it makes you feel any different'...Well, she didn't that night, but when she took E the first time, she was with me, and she was sick, really sick, and she's never touched it since..."

Another woman, Kirsty (a 20 year old student who is a light user) was clear in her own mind that Ecstasy was "good", but less clear on how to express this to somebody else. Eventually, she decided to tell the interested:

"...originally, I told them it initially makes you feel really happy, em...it's like being in love. Then it becomes a bit like going for a shag for one night. You might get a good shag: you might not. You've just got to take that risk. So that's what I use now..."

Richie (a 30 year old employed light user) claimed actually to regret being asked by for his opinion by intending users. As he put it:

"It's none of my business...I'm not a disciple for any particular drug. I'm not a disciple or messiah for any drug...That's people's own business if they take it. If they ask me, I'll say what I think about it, but I would never turn anybody onto a drug. It may not be for them, and I don't want to be responsible for fucking them up..."

The three that had introduced more than 7 other people to Ecstasy were long term users, who had used a lot of Ecstasy over a use career of between 5 and 8 years. One was a self-confessed one-time dealer, for whom "introduced" had a different meaning. Of the other two, one had evangelised about Ecstasy in the *"..early days.."* when he was *"naive"* but thought he was *"wide"*, and that Ecstasy was the answer to all life's problems. The third, Fraser (a 43 year old employee who is now a light user) also recalled what he referred to as *"...the initial E scene.."*. He continued:

"...probably far too many...I don't really make a habit of it now, of evangelising, ah...people for drug use...but if I go back to talk about the initial E scene, yeah, if you were out on the E scene then, with a group of people, all taking E...everybody... it took a while before I realised that it was...it could be quite a selfish drug really..."

Networks of Users

All were then asked how many of their friends were Ecstasy users. In brief, the light users tended to say that *"some"* of their friends were users; the medium users that *"most"* were, and the heavy users that *"all"* were. Many light users indicated that, for various reasons, and at least for them, they had fewer Ecstasy using friends now than had previously been the case. As Fraser (a 43 year old employed light user) said:

"Well, at one point in my life, yeah, when I was taking E on a regular basis, you know, nearly everybody I knew would have been taking it…but now, there are a handful of those that I still see on a regular basis, and of those, very, very few are doing E….I mean the scene is old, and the bubble's burst…"

Another, Sharon (a 19 year old employed light user) commented similarly that, *"most of my friends don't now: but we did. We've kind of fell away from all that scene now. We don't tend to do as much of that now, but, I suppose, when we did, everyone did, yeah."*

With the medium and heavy users, a few agreed that their current consumption (and that of their friends) might now be lower than it might have been at its peak, but this was because of the currently low quality of purchasable Ecstasy, rather than a declining desire to take it. As Willie (a 24 year old unemployed heavy user) put it:

"Most of my friends still do it, to some extent, yeah…but it's died out a bit, just because there's no good quality E about. It's not worth it. As far as I'm concerned, in Glasgow, it's no good…they were bringing it back from Holland, but that's stopped about a year ago, so I won't buy any now. I'd much rather take a bit of coke and smack together…a wee line of each, you know: it's cheaper and you're guaranteed a good one…not like this horrible cocktail which doesn't make you feel too great afterwards, which a lot of these home made Eees do…"

What is striking is that Ecstasy seems to be a drug that people can enjoy intensely at first, although in various different ways, but one that users come to have a more cautious view of as they discover that every Ecstasy experience is not necessarily as good – or as bad – as the first. In the next chapter we consider what types of Ecstasy seem to exist, and, indeed, what types of user. Crucially, we examine the evidence on tolerance and addiction to Ecstasy.

NOTES

[4]   Early use in Britain is documented in Person, G., Ditton, J., Newcombe, R. & Gilman, M., "'Everything starts with an "E"': An introduction to ecstasy use by young people in Britain", **Druglink**, 1991, 6 (6): 10–11.

[5]   Technical detail is in Forsyth, A., "Places and patterns of drug use in the Scottish dance scene", **Addiction**, 1996, 91 (4): 511–521.

[6]   Beck, J. & Rosenbaum, M., **Pursuit of Ecstasy: The MDMA Experience**, SUNY Press, New York, 1994.

[7]   Technical detail is in Smith, I., Suddle, A., Gallagher, D., Ditton, J. & Hammersley, R., "The absence of chronic psychiatric problems following MDMA ("ecstasy") use", **Drug and Alcohol Dependence**, (forthcoming, 2000).

[8]   Technical detail is in two articles. First, Cooper. G., Allen, D., Scott, K., Oliver, J., Ditton, J. & Smith, I., "Hair analysis: Self-reported use of "speed" and "ecstasy" compared with laboratory findings", **Journal of Forensic Science**, 2000, 45 (2): 400–406. Second, Ditton, J., Cooper, G., Scott, K., Allen, D., Oliver, J.& Smith, I.,"Hair testing for "ecstasy" in a large volunteer sample of Scottish drug users", **Addiction Biology**, 2000, 5: 207–213.

[9]   See: Ditton, J. & Hammersley, R. **A Very Greedy Drug: Cocaine in Context**, Harwood Academic Press, Reading, 1996.

[10] Technical detail is in a book chapter written by Ditton, J., Hammersley. R. & Smith, I., and entitled, "'New' drugs, crime, and the informal economy", in J. Shapland, H-J. Albrecht, J. Ditton and T. Godefroy (eds) **The Informal Economy: Threat and Opportunity in the City**, Max Planck Institut, Freiburg, 2000.

[11] And full technical detail can be found in our article, "Patterns of ecstasy use by drug users", written by Hammersley, R., Ditton, J., Smith, I. & Short, E., and published in the **British Journal of Criminology**, 1999, 39 (4): 625–647.

[12] See the articles cited in footnote 2, *supra*.

[13] It is not clear what "gouch" means here, as "gouching" normally refers to sedation, which is not what you would expect from amphetamines.

[14] Nipping is "necking" to use an old-fashioned term.

[15] 'Gouchy" comes from "gouching" which means to be in an almost unconscious, highly sedated and relaxed state after using heroin, or similar drugs. As we will see, the opposite of "gouchy" is "bouncy', when someone is high, elated and "bouncing all over the place.'

[16] The term "ned" is widely used in Glasgow. It is a derogatory word for young, working class people, particularly boys, who tend to dress in whatever casual gear is currently fashionable (often tracksuits etc, but fashions change over the years) and have a reputation for being rowdy, badly behaved, criminal and violent. "Ned" is something you call other people, a type you identify primarily by appearance (but accent and behaviour play a part also). Working class Glaswegians also refer to people who are "hard as nails', not necessarily "tough" but with absolutely no soft edges or refinement about them. Neds might be "hard as nails", but it is a relative term, and who is a "ned" depends of course on how you see yourself. When not reporting direct speech we will use the term "casual" which refers less judgementally to a dress style (often associated with "neddishness').

CHAPTER TWO
Types of Ecstasy User

A staple in drug research is the classification of users into types. Below we outline why we had great difficulty with this. As did members of our small group:

"...every kind. I don't think there's a particular kind of person. How would I describe an E user? Just your average person ..." (Kirsty)

"Och! Don't know. They vary. Any type. Anybody ..." (Phil)

"I don't really think there's a ... it's completely widespread across all sorts of groups and classes and sexes and the age groups ..." (Liz)

"...students take it, so do academics, so do lots of folk, so do criminals, so do junkies, so do drugs workers ..." (Richie)

"people that come from a not so good up-bringing ... and then you've got your people that have gone to private school ..." (Danny)

"...full-timers and part-timers, you know, people that do it all the time and people that don't ..." (Kath)

"...those that take it, and take tons of it, and those that take it in control ..." (Gael)

"...people that are into rave music, and, you know, people who aren't ..." (Iain)

"...you get your sort of younger generation, you know, young folk, late teens, early 20s sort of crowd ... and then there's the sort of older ones ..." (Stuart)

"...you've got your dealer that takes it every weekend ... you get the occasional user who takes it every now and then, and you get your guys that take it every month ..." (Euan)

TYPOLOGIES OF ECSTASY USE

In the main sample, all respondents were asked in an open-ended way, "what types of Ecstasy user are there?" near the end of each interview. This can be useful in helping to develop typologies of users. However, we obtained almost as many native typologies as we had respondents. Here are some sample responses taken only from the small group:

Sandra (a 24 year old employed medium level user):
- People who do it all the time – nutters and neds. Tend to be younger
- People who do it occasionally. Quite responsible with it. Tend to be older.
- Those who take it less often

Fraser (a 43 year old employed light user):
- Generic – right across the board
- A lot of the young team
- A lot of 30-somethings
- A few ex-hippies. Not so many. A bit thin on the ground

Tam (a 16 year old unemployed light user)
- People who take it because everybody else is taking it and they want to enjoy themselves at the dancing

Naomi (a 23 year old employed light user)
- People that use it to enhance an evening (non-regular users)
- People that can't have a good time without it
- People who just use it when going to the pub

Agnes (a 20 year old employed medium level user)
- Just everybody

Morag (a 22 year old employed medium level user)
- Lawyers, doctors
- Right wing fascists
- A broad spectrum of people

Charlie (a 22 year old unemployed ex-user)
- People who don't treat it with respect
- People who do
- People who have stopped because they believe it is physically destructive
- People who think it's not really a drug

Moira (a 19 year old unemployed heavy user)
- People who sit down
- People who are greedy
- People who dance

From a taxonomic point of view some of these, particularly Charlie's, recall the wonderful Chinese classification of animals quoted in the Preface to Foucault's classic 1966 book, *The Order of Things*, wherein animals are divided into: (a) belonging to the Emperor, (b) embalmed, (c) tame, (d) sucking pigs, (e) sirens, (f) fabulous, (g) stray dogs, (h) included in the present classification, (i) frenzied, (j) innumerable, (k) drawn with a very fine camel hair brush, (l) *et cetera*, (m) having just broken the water pitcher, (n) that from a long way off look like flies!

Yet, this does not mean that such typologies don't help during fieldwork, and even during the data analysis stage. At the fieldwork stage, the typologies provided were compared to the structure of the emerging sample. The comparison between what types of user we seemed to be interviewing, and what types of user respondents thought existed allowed us to define certain types as saturated, and the search for more members of such types was discontinued. As new types emerged from regular analysis of user's nominations, they were targeted for future recruitment and interview.

So far, Ecstasy users, both in the large sample and in the small group, have only been simply classified into light, medium and heavy users in terms of how many Ecstasy tablets they had consumed in the year prior to interview. Simply *level* of use, such as this, is often seen as adequate itself, and indeed, so far, has been here. However, we were also able to distinguish two different *patterns* of use. Because data had been obtained for each respondent relating both to the number of days that Ecstasy was consumed during each month, and for each day of use how many tablets were consumed on average, it was possible to distinguish "stable" users from "erratic" ones at each level. Essentially, a stable user was one who tended to use the same amount of Ecstasy the same number of days each month, while an erratic user tended to have different patterns of use during different months.

Native Typologies

When the large sample was complete, the typologies had another use: it was possible to see if those with different levels and patterns of Ecstasy use preferred different typologies of Ecstasy user. In examination of the native typologies, it became clear that they fell into one or other of four broad types. Respondents were not limited to a fixed number of types: 58 (25%) of respondents just chose one word answers ("everybody" was by far the most frequent); 53 (23%) specified two types; 80 (35%) three types; 30 (13%) four types; 5 (2%) five types; and 3 (1%) six or more types.

Most frequent was classification of users by type of person (72 respondents, 31% of the large sample, did it this way). These ranged from the fairly simple (one respondent just said "neds", another "the young, and the old"), through to increasingly complex typologies such as "oldies, students and kids", and "neds, hippies, ravers and skateboarders", with one respondent (a 21 year old female employed graduate) giving the quite complicated typology of "ravers, occasional users, late teenagers, the unemployed, students, clubbers and addicts".

A close second was classification of users by frequency of use, which was chosen by 66 (29%) of respondents. Again these ranged in sophistication, from "those who do it every weekend, and those who just do it occasionally", through "casual users, regular users and druggies", to "those who just try it once, those who only do it occasionally, those who do it at weekends, and addicts".

Third were the 48 (21%) who claimed that there were not types, as such, as just "everybody" took Ecstasy; or, rather more precisely, that those who use Ecstasy just couldn't be classified.

Finally, a smaller number of respondents (43, 19% of the total sample) classified users by the type of use to which Ecstasy was put. These typologies were rather more sophisticated and thoughtful, and are thus worth considering in more detail. Some were quite rough and ready ("users and abusers", "hedonists and clubbers", "the occasional and the obsessed", "the recreational and the depressed", "people who take it to fit in and people who like it", and "folk who take it to have a good time and folk who take it to escape reality") but others were considerably more detailed. Examples are from one respondent from the large sample who claimed:

"...people who take it to transcend everyday life spiritually, people who take it for kicks as part of a group coming of age thing, people

who start off like that but don't give up or grow up, obnoxious people, conservative people who live in the West End and moved there to punish their parents, people who try to make it a way of life, and those who use it as a sexual stimulant ..."

Another large sample respondent put it like this:

"...people that take it because they don't have a social life, E becomes part of their social life, and they don't feel comfortable out socialising without being on E. A few who take it for spiritual reasons. None who inject hard drugs. Stupid people – you get them everywhere – even more stupid when on drugs. And then there's people who dabble, like me, who add E to the occasional night out, but who don't want E to become an essential part of it ..."

But is there any link between the different ways of self typologising users, and our typological mix of level (light, medium and heavy) and pattern of use (stable or erratic)? In the large sample, the 201 past year Ecstasy using respondents were classified into one of 6 groups: 41 light stable users, 42 light erratic users; 25 medium stable users, 48 medium erratic users; 23 heavy stable users and 22 heavy erratic users. There was no relationship between type of preferred typology and level or pattern of use (separately or in combination). Table 2.1 has the detail.

There is no relationship between level/pattern and self-typology, although it is noticeable that types of people typologies are not only

NATIVE TYPOLOGIES AND LEVELS AND PATTERNS OF ECSTASY USE				
(n)	Frequency %	Use type %	People type %	Everybody %
Non-users + ex-users (28)	18	11	39	32
Light stable (41)	20	24	37	20
Light erratic (42)	43	17	24	17
Medium stable (25)	40	16	24	20
Medium erratic (48)	25	23	33	19
Heavy stable (23)	35	9	30	26
Heavy erratic (22)	23	27	32	18
ALL (229)	**29**	**19**	**31**	**21**

Table 2.1

most popular overall, but are also most popular among non-users and
ex-users, light stable users, and medium erratic and heavy erratic users.
Frequency typologies are most popular among light erratic users,
medium stable ones and heavy stable users. Excluding the non-users
and ex-users (and, for the time being, the light users for whom discern-
ing a pattern isn't always easy) medium and heavy stable users tend to
see Ecstasy users in terms of frequency typologies, and medium and
heavy erratic users in terms of types of people.

The Small Group Again

In the small group of 22, 5 could be classified as light stable users
(Tam, Kirsty, Gael, Naomi and Stuart), 5 as light erratic users (Sharon,
Euan, Danny, Richie and Fraser); 3 as medium stable users (Agnes,
Morag and Sandra), 2 as medium erratic users (Liz and Iain); 3 as
heavy stable users (Moira, Kath and Fiona) and 3 as heavy erratic ones
(Phil, Douglas and Willie). One respondent – Charlie – had used no
Ecstasy in the year prior to quantitative interview. Of the 22, 11 were
male and 11 female. Although a small group, the 22 members of it
were selected specifically to cover each of the 6 level/pattern types
(although the degree to which they represent each type is unknowable).
They can also help illustrate the ways that Ecstasy users typologise
each other.

Each was asked to say what types of Ecstasy user existed, but most
had difficulty in answering with any precision. Some were puzzled by
the question, as was Kirsty, the 20 year old student who herself was a
light stable user: "*every kind. I don't think there's a particular kind of
person. How would I describe an E user? Just your average person*",
or Phil, the 19 year old employee who was a heavy erratic user
himself: "*Och! Don't know. They vary. Any type. Anybody*". Others
apparently thought the same way, but were more specific, as was Liz,
the 19 year old employee who was a medium erratic Ecstasy user
herself:

"*I don't really think there's a … From what I can see, I think it's completely widespread across all sorts of groups and classes and sexes and
the age groups. I mean, I know people who are sort of late 20s professional people who earn a lot of money … sort of almost yuppies, who
are taking it, and I know 16 year olds who are taking it and going to
raves. I know students who are taking it. Male, female, working class,
very middle class. I think it's completely widespread. I don't think
there are any definable groups who take it …*"

Some resisted mentally picturing an Ecstasy user in the same way as they could picture, for example, a heroin user. Richie, a 30 year old employee who was a light erratic Ecstasy user put it like this:

"One of the curious things ... is that Ecstasy has kind of, sort of made it much more difficult to categorise people in terms of taking. I could answer the question, what does a particular person that takes smack look like? Well, he's got a car radio under his arm, he's covered in spots and he's got his granny on his tail ... but people take E in various ways: it cuts across your question. ... Students take it, so do academics, so do lots of folk, so do criminals, so do junkies, so do drugs workers. In terms of patterns of use, I couldn't tell you. I suspect that it has now become, not so much widespread, that's a bit alarmist, but there's so many different groups, categories of people that use it, that the notion of categorising people I think now is redundant ..."

Part of the received culture of taking Ecstasy is that it is a great leveller. That is, the feelings of happiness, contentment and empathy combine on the dance floor with the feelings of high energy to dissolve the traditional boundaries separating classes, sexes and ages. Danny, a 21 year old employee who was a light erratic Ecstasy user himself, recalled:

"We used to go to some clubs, and you'd have someone from Easterhouse[17] come up to you and they'd shake your hand and say, 'Alright, man? What have you taken?' ... I mean I didn't like that at all. Because I don't know the guy, you don't just go up to someone and go, 'Right, man?' ... If you did that outside when you were straight during the day, you'd get a kicking ... The only thing we had in common was that he was on E and I was on E, and we happened to be in the same club, that's all. The next day when he's straight and I'm straight, we'd have nothing in common ..."

Most attempts to respond to this question appear to be different ways of illustrating the classlessness, agelessness and sexlessness of users, rather than the provision of actual taxonomies. For example, *"people that come from a not so good up-bringing ... and then you've got your people that have gone to private school ..."* (Danny, again), or, *"full-timers and part-timers, you know, people that do it all the time and people that don't ..."* (Kath, a 20 year old employed female who was a light stable Ecstasy user), or, *"those that take it, and take tons of it, and those that take it in control"* (Gael, the 25 year old employee who was a heavy stable Ecstasy user), or, *"people that are into rave music, and, you know, people who aren't"* (Iain, a 20 year old employee who was a medium erratic user) or, finally, *"you get your sort of younger generation, you know, young folk, late teens, early 20s sort of crowd ... and then there's the sort of older ones"* (Stuart, a 28 year old student who was a light stable Ecstasy user).

One or two based their response on classifications derived from frequency of use (*"you've got your dealer that takes it every weekend ... you get the occasional user who takes it every now and then, and you get your guys that take it every month ..."* – from Euan, a 27 year old employee who was a light erratic Ecstasy user himself); with Naomi, a 23 year old employee who was a light stable user, combining both frequency and regularity of use in a way reminiscent of our classification by level and pattern of use:

"Em ... some who take it occasionally when they're drunk; there's ones who maybe take it occasionally planned for a big night out ... occasionally not planned ... em ... there's ones who take it every week, and there's ones who take a lot a week ... I know some people who take 6 tablets when they're going out. They maybe don't take it every week, but when they do go out, and they want to get out of it, they take a lot of drugs ..."

Overall, however, what is most noticeable from both the responses of the large sample and from the small group is the sheer difficulty that most respondents had in offering any sense that there is a type of person who typifies the Ecstasy user, or any type of person for whom Ecstasy is (and is not) sometimes or often the drug of choice. In a classificatory sense, Ecstasy seems truly "classless".

"BOUNCY" E OR "GOUCHY" E?

Types of Tablet

In the small group, two of the respondents (first Moira, a 19 year old unemployed heavy stable Ecstasy user; and second, Charlie the ex-user, who was 22 years old, and unemployed) answered the question about "types of Ecstasy user" by saying:

"There's people that prefer bouncy E, and there's people that prefer likes of doves that are, like, gouchy. Most of my pals prefer gouchy, which I can't understand, because they just sit there like flabbering wrecks; but I mean like me and my best mate, we prefer stuff that can sort of get you up ..."

and Charlie:

"There's the people who use it to go down, and there's the people who use it to go up ..."

Beliefs that some tablets sold as Ecstasy were adulterated with non-psychoactive substances (*"vim"* and *"flour"* were mentioned, and as one user put it, *"some of them are rubbish and some of them are great"*) flowed imperceptibly into beliefs that some tablets sold as Ecstasy did not contain Ecstasy at all (*"the doves these days just aren't any good ... I think the folk that are producing them have just manufactured the dove stamp so that anyone can just make doves now"*), into beliefs that tablets sold as Ecstasy also contained other psychoactive substances (additions included *"heroin"*, *"speed"*, *"LSD"*, *"coke"*, *"mescaline"*), and from there into ideas that there were different types of Ecstasy itself.

Ecstasy seems to have been the first drug overtly named as such as a marketing ploy. The current number of different sub-brand names is simply staggering: our large sample was able to recall, between them, an average of 9 different types each, and recalled a total of 108 different sub-brands that they had consumed, again between them, in the previous year alone.

The names speak for themselves, so all we have done is categorise them. "Pills" use names that belong in some sense to other pills or tablets. "Descriptive" names describe the appearance of the E in some general way. This includes "Squares", which was a generic name for lots of different brands of Ecstasy. The other most common kind was "Doves", so called because they have the image of a dove stamped on them. Some of the other "People and Animals" category may describe the stamp or picture on the tablet, others are more metaphorical or whimsical. "Effect" names seem to divide neatly into the magical, names that suggest that Ecstasy "does you in", and science fiction names. "Place" names all suggest places associated with Ecstasy or dance culture. The M25 London orbital motorway was the access route for the major unlicensed raves in the late 1980s because when a rave's location was announced on the night, the M25 was used to get there quickly. "Food & Drink" names is the largest category and worth subdividing. Some of these may describe the tablet, or a logo on it, others may be more poetic. Finally, there is an inevitable list of "Other" names that do not fit our somewhat arbitrary taxonomy.

PILLS
bayer
blue heart
pellet
purple heart
white caps

DESCRIPTIVE
amber
Big white one
blue and white
China split
China white
dimples
globe
ovals
red and black
red and yellow
smoothies
Squares
tiddleiwink

PEOPLE AND
ANIMALS
dove
super dove
adam & eve
eve
dennis the menace
EVA
greyhound
malcolm X
man united
mickey mouse
pink panther
robin

saddam hussein
superman
wee boy

EFFECTS
magic white
magic cube
flatliner
head fucker
little bastard
madman
shocker
SF
speed bomb
rockets
flying saucer
bermuda triangle

PLACES
M25
New Yorker
Pink New Yorker
Californian
Sunrise
Amsterdammer
Milky Way

FOOD AND
DRINK FRUIT:
banana split
rhubarb and
custard
strawberry
snowball
mini snowball
pink snowball

snowman
disco biscuit
brown biscuit
white biscuit
grey biscuit
rusk
disco burger
coke burger
yellow burger
love hearts
parma violet
B52s
blue lagoon
Lemon & Lime
maddog
salt and pepper

OTHER
bee bops
black jack
cartoon
clog
diamond
double barrel
e130
EA
fantasy
foreign E
phase 4
pink barrel
PT
shamrock
triple X
undergrounds

The poetic profusion of names, and the images they evoke. is striking. What is one to make of a drug that can be anything from Malcolm X to a banana split, or anything from a dove to a headfucker? Both users of Ecstasy and their Ecstasy experiences are extremely diverse and this is reflected in the diversity of names for the drug.

Change Over Time

Back to the small group, some referred back to years before the interview when, apparently, there was only one type of Ecstasy, and that it was of high quality, and that adulteration and substitution were relatively recent phenomena. Consider the remarks of Fraser, a 43 year old employee who is now a light erratic user:

"In terms of what's been available on the market over the last four or five years, it is quite a range. I mean, for me, my initial experience for about the first three months ... the drugs that were being made by people that had, they knew what they were doing. I think it was, eh ... people that had either worked for the pharmaceutical industry or something, so there was a very very high quality of tablet, and it was a very pure experience. After that the quality went down hill fairly rapidly. Yeah, there were some that were just ... maybe, I'm not sure if it's a difficult chemical formula to get right, but often it would just seem to be slightly off, or else there seemed to be other drugs mixed in there, or there were other drugs that they were making: it might be MDEA or MDA. Or else it could have been cut with speed or coke or even downers, even, I mean ... smack ..."

It transpires, from examining the responses to questions relating to types of Ecstasy, that – almost universally with this group – available Ecstasy comes in these two forms: "doves" which seem to generate feelings of de-energised contentment, and are "gouchy"; and "squares" which are variously defined as "trippy", "smacky" and "heavy" and which foster the energy needed for dancing for long periods. It is also believed that tablet strength varies. A few examples:

"I prefer the, well, almost speedy light E ... that's I don't like the ones that are heavy and smacky, I like the ones that sort of give you a wee bit of energy and make you dance and things ..." (Naomi, the 23 year old employee who is a light stable Ecstasy user)

"Some you get are quite gouchy; and some you get are quite speedy. It depends on what it has in them. Em ... with some, you're more alert: you're more aware of what you're doing, and you're more in control ... In other ones, there is more control of you: you're just sat in a corner all night and you cannae move. I do believe that some you take are stronger than others. I've heard people say, 'I've took one, and it hardly done anything. And I took half of another one another week, and I was totally away with it' ... so there must be stronger ones and weaker ones ..." (Agnes, a 20 year old employee who is a medium stable user)

"The doves make you feel just very very smiley and happy, but you don't have much energy. Other ones that I had recently that people have called squares, I don't know what the term is ... they tend to be a lot more ... I don't know, they feel a lot more smacky. You're more fucked, if I can use that expression. It's not so much that you feel happy ... it's ... it's ... more like acid. It's a lot more ... you're tenser when you're coming up. You feel completely disoriented, like you're tripping. You can't hear what people are saying, and the music goes all funny ..." (Liz, a 19 year old employee who is a medium erratic user)

"Squares keep you up longer, where a dove is a goucher. Squares give you a sort of acidy type of trip ... Doves are like heavier, like you cannae keep your eyes open, like you find your eyes flickering. I can't find the energy to get up ... I find myself staggering about on them ..."

(Moira, the 19 year old unemployed heavy stable user)

All this suggests a drug that can have very varied effects on people. Why might this be? It is not plausible that different brands of Ecstasy contain different chemicals, or have different effects. Ecstasy basically works by stimulating the receptors of one of the main brain neuro-transmitter systems – the serotonin system. This stimulation seems to lead to a depletion of serotonin afterwards. Serotonin is involved in many behaviours, notably depression. Indeed, modern anti-depressants are SSRI's or "Selective serotonin re-uptake inhibitors", which try to reduce the depletion of serotonin. It is more likely that how users are affected depends on how they were feeling beforehand, and the situation they are in when they are using Ecstasy, but as we will see in Chapter 3, users made more of the fact that Ecstasy tended to cheer them up, however they had been feeling.

It is plausible that Ecstasy has different effects depending upon the existing state of the user. People who are already "up for it", feeling good and "ready to party" may have high levels of serotonin in their brains, so when they take Ecstasy it is possible for it to have lots of effect and stimulate them. People who want to chill, relax or mellow out, or are even depressed, may have less serotonin in their brains, so when they take Ecstasy it may have different effects. Perhaps it does not stimulate them, but instead reduces activity as it quickly depletes the limited available serotonin further.

If this is correct, then different brands only have their different effects because people selectively choose different brands depending on whether they want to "gouch" or "bounce", which in turn depends on their current mood, which is related to their serotonin levels.

CONSUMPTION AND TOLERANCE

Here, all the data comes from the small group.

Consumption

As for consumption, a simple distinction can be made: the erratic users tend to take whatever Ecstasy they are going to take in any one night all in one go; the stable users take their tablets sequentially.

Light stable users claim to typically take half a tablet – at least initially. Gael (a 20 year old employee) felt that a half was insufficient, even unpleasant, but that taking the other half helped:

"I found that a half just wasn't enough. Usually, I tend to go on a bit of a downer on a half. I'd have a whitey[18] on a half because I wasn't properly Eeed. I was a bit out of my nut, but I was still a bit straight. So I think when you're in that sort of state, you can sort of fight it a bit ... [but] ... as soon as I take another half, then I'm just too Eeed to sort of think about it ..."

All the light stable users said roughly the same thing. Another (Stuart, the 28 year old student) commented, *"take a half ... feel it coming up, then take another half. It lasts longer, and you don't get such bad side effects ..."*. The light erratic users, on the other hand, even though their annual intake might not be any different to that of the light stable users, could all remember times when they had far exceeded their normal dose. Fraser, a 43 year old employee, recalled:

"...at the height of it, yes ... I think the most I ever took was perhaps three and a half on one occasion ... greed probably: just trying to experience as much pleasure out of it as possible ..."

He was extreme: most of the light erratic users could only remember the odd occasion when they had taken two tablets at once. Euan, a 27 year old employee, put it like this:

"I have done ... [more than one a night] ... I've taken up to two a night ... because you're already high and happy on the first one, and you've had a few drinks, and you're willing to take a second one ... I try to keep to it if I get an E ... just to take half of it, because if you start taking it all in one, then your tolerance builds up on it, and I'm not prepared to spend loads and loads of money to get the same effect as just one E. That's just stupid ..."

The medium stable users are much like the light stable users: they take a half, or perhaps one, but they do so more often. The medium erratic users might start with one tablet, then add to that as the evening wears on. Sandra, a 24 year old employee:

"The maximum I would ever take is one and a half in a night. Em ... I would usually take the whole one first, and then after about 2 or 3 hours, I would take a half. I would never, I have never taken one and a half together ... I suppose it's maybe financial. I couldn't afford to do that every weekend ..."

Another (Iain, a 20 year old employee) had ratcheted the dose up slightly:

"I usually do it in ones. I'll take one, and then I'll take another one, and then I'll reach the stage that I'll take another half. ... They last longer when you first take it. When you first take an E, it lasts 4 or 5 hours, and as your body gets used to it, it doesn't last as long. So, the first time, you'll be out of your face for hours, the second time, you'll be our of your face for two hours ... So, that's why you take more, to make it last longer. It's not to get any more mad with it: it's just to make it last longer ..."

The heavy stable users space out their intake, but can end up consuming more, as they are pacing themselves with halves taken regularly, or with single tablets taken less often. Fiona, the 27 year old employee:

"Sometimes I take more than one a night. I tend to do binges and then come off it. It's always just the weekend though, it's never during the week. Well, it's not that much of a binge. It's just, like, 3 or 4 over a weekend, and then I'm back to one. I tend to take a half every hour, and you can stay at this plane if I'm doing that. But Saturday there, I took two in a whack … but that's not what I usually do. Normally, it's half every hour …"

A 19 year old unemployed heavy stable user did much the same. Moira:

"I used to take between like 1 and 4 … I always take it in halves. I just don't go swally [take them all at once]. I mean, a lot of folk do that, but I just find that too heavy, then you go, 'Wow! what's happening!' … I would take a half, wait until that comes up on me, and then like once it's beginning to wear off, take another half … you know, just keep it going throughout the night … keep the buzz going. It's just a half, and then it's about an hour and a half later. It depends on the E as well, though. Some last longer, I mean, squares last longer than doves … I usually take 4 at the max. Usually it's about 2. If I'm going to a rave, I'll take three with me, but I usually only take two through the night as I've usually got speed as well …"

She continued:

"Right, so I'm going to a rave. Say I've got two E with me, right, and a half or a quarter ounce of speed … I'll eat some on the bus, you know. So … em … the bus going to a rave, I'll take some and I like the speed buzz, so I'll get a really good buzz out of my speed first before I'll start taking E, then maybe take half an E, and then take half a bag of sulph, then half an E and then half a bag of sulph … and usually keep a wee bit of sulph for the end of the night and the bus journey home, so I don't fall asleep, so I can go to a party then … start drinking. I usually have a half bottle of vodka, usually get a half bottle of vodka. I went through a really shady patch a wee while ago and I drank loads … but now I stick to my half bottle and that's me happy …"

At this level, the erratic users did not differ much from the stable ones, except, perhaps in the other drugs they used to maintain the desired level of intoxication. Willie, the 24 year old unemployed man:

"I used to always take about three in a night. Probably now I'd only do about one and a half or two maybe. I'd half a good one, and go halfers on another, or get one for free in the club. You know, if someone were to buy it for you. I would be more inclined to spend my money on good coke, if I could get it at the dancing ... I would take one, and then another one within a couple of hours of each other so that you're peaking all the time ... and then take snorts of coke sort of every 45 minutes or an hour, you know, to keep you buzzing ..."

Tolerance

Unsurprisingly, perhaps, the heavier a person's Ecstasy use, the more likely that he or she is likely to believe that users can build up a tolerance for Ecstasy. Light users tended to think tolerance was a possibility, but not for them. This 20 year old student (Kirsty) who was a light stable user, was typical:

"I don't think I do it enough to build up a tolerance, but I think ... yeah, I think ... I don't know. Maybe you don't build up a tolerance. Maybe you just get used to the feeling. Maybe want to try more, or something. I really don't know ..."

Although one or two of the light erratic users rejected the idea entirely. This is Richie, the 30 year old employed light erratic user:

"See what I was talking about earlier on? ... about sort of topping up doses, that lasts as long as your inclination to ... possibly I'm speaking personally here, but I've never had the notion of the next night go back and take more, the next night go back and take more ... next night go back and take more. I don't see any necessity to keep taking more in order to get the effect you started off with. I think it's more unusual and it's more subtle than that ... If you're not content with the effect it has, then you're either a glutton or you're a fairly dull person, I suspect ..."

Medium level users were much more likely to agree that Ecstasy could generate tolerance, but more because of effects-greed than because of pharmacological dependency. Here, it becomes an issue of control rather than of chemicals, as with this 20 year old employed medium stable user, Agnes:

"Aye, I'd say there is a tolerance, but again, I'd say you start to control it more, and then greed comes in so you want more because you, like, get used to the feeling so you want it a bit stronger. But I wouldn't say that it's totally addictive. No, because it's not as if you have a problem stopping ..."

Other medium level Ecstasy users were also users of other drugs, and they could use these other experiences to put their Ecstasy use into perspective. As Liz, a 19 year old employed medium erratic user put it, *"I've definitely got a tolerance to hash, and I have probably developed a tolerance to speed as well. But, I mean, I've taken both those drugs a lot more regularly than I would take Ecstasy."*

Heavy users were adamant. For them, tolerance was a reality – albeit one only experienced by other people. First Kath, a 25 year old employee, and then Moira, 19 years old and unemployed. They were both heavy stable users:

"One of my friends, he got to the stage where he was going to raves and he was taking 6 in a night, and he couldn't get a hit off it. He started off just like us, he started taking one, but he was going out every week, we were going out once or twice a month. He was going out every weekend. Friday, Saturday night. Started off one, then it was two, then it was three, then it was four. Then he was going to raves and then he was taking 6 and 7, and his body became that way where it just wasn't getting a hit off it. He just stopped taking it altogether for a year, and he started back on it four months ago, and he started getting hits off it without taking as many ..."

Now Moria:

"Definitely! ... I know this guy who was, like he started taking an E, then it was three, and then it went up to six. You know, like he would take an E, and he'd be getting a buzz out of it for half an hour, whereas I'd be taking one and it would do me for a good few hours ... But ... em ... I think that might be partly due to people's build, you know, their body weight, and stuff. I don't know, it may be something to do with that ..."

In sum, there is no belief in dependency (in the sense of needing to take Ecstasy once some sort of pain of withdrawal has set in) but there is a common belief in the possibility of getting to a stage where greed has overtaken control. Insofar as this is believed, it is believed to be reversible.

Does Price Affect Use?

However, for most, greed is not believed to be price-determined. Each interviewee was asked if he or she would take more Ecstasy if it was cheaper. For most, reducing or eliminating the cost of Ecstasy would not increase use. Exceptions are some of the light users, who are only in that category because of poverty. As Tam (the 16 year old unemployed man) put it, "*I'm not working at the moment, so I'm not doing it very often at the moment*". Other light users rejected the possibility out of hand. Danny (a 21 year old employee) had actual experience of cheaper Ecstasy, and it didn't change his view:

"*No … I mean I've got it offered at half price at the weekend there, and I didn't take more of it … I'm just not into it like that … like to be more in control …*"

He suggested that ideally, even if Ecstasy were free, he would only take it "*maybe every three months*". Indeed, this was typical. Even when pressed, and offered imaginary free Ecstasy, most said things like: "*if it was really good, and free, once every 6 months, or something like that …*" or, "*once every couple of months … I'm quite happy with the way I do it now*", and, "*If it was free? Well, not knowing entirely what it does to you, probably not more than, I don't know, once a month maybe?*", finally, "*I think once every 6 weeks. If it was free and it was good quality, once every 6 weeks or so would be fine*".

With heavier users, the erratic/stable distinction re-emerges. The stable users were all quite definite that they would not take more, but the erratic ones were less sure. These two medium erratic users (Liz, the 19 year old employee, and Iain, a 20 year old employee) would both use more if it was cheaper, but insist that they would stay in control:

"*Yeah … if it was free, I mean, I don't know. I think that I have a sensible attitude because I think that I know that I have to get up for work on Monday morning, and I like to think that I've got a life and that I'm fairly together and I also like to have a good time ... but I do confine that pretty much to the weekends, so I look on Ecstasy as a way of enhancing my social life. It's not like ... my life or anything, and I don't think that if it was free, or I could just walk into a shop and buy it, that I would just go and sit in a bed-sit and do that all day, because I would not enjoy my life. I suppose that if it was half the price it is now, that is, it if was seven pounds fifty a tab, I would probably buy more in that I would spend that money anyway, if you know what I mean. But if it was free ... available on the street corner ... that doesn't mean that I would take it every day because I wouldn't ..."*

As Iain put it:

"Probably not, because I know what it takes to get me into the state that I want to be in ... I think I would just take what I usually take in the dancing, although if I was up on Sunday, and it was cheaper and easier to get hold of, I'd probably take more during the day ... If it was cheaper, I would probably buy more ... but it would be spaced out over more time, like start the next day rather than take loads in the space of three hours, or something. ... I'd go to the dancing, I'd take it ... then Sunday, I'd spread it out the whole day Sunday ... but stop at 6 or 7 o'clock, because I know I've got to go back to work on the Monday ..."

All the heavy stable users emphatically denied they would increase their use if the price fell, but the heavy erratic users felt that their consumption would probably increase, although their pattern of consumption would not alter. Willie, a 24 year old unemployed man, however, felt that he might initially celebrate the fall in price before returning to previous consumption levels:

"Eh, I would ... I'm not going to lie and say that I wouldn't ... but I would, I definitely would. If it was free ... how often would I take it? ... I would, right? ... but after say, a week, I would cut down just to the weekends because I'm due at my work, and I know that if I got full of it every night, full of Eccy, I would be in no fit state to go to my work, so I couldn't do it ... so it would end up being the same as now, only it would be taking more at weekends ..."

All of the interviewees denied ever committing any crime to finance their use of Ecstasy (although Stuart, a 28 year old student who was a light erratic user admitted, *"just apart from, like, defrauding the government, you know, the usual sort of stuff that everybody does to live. Just the usual, but not like mugging old grannies or anything like that, or breaking into places"*) except one who confessed to dealing in Ecstasy, to having stolen to purchase opiates in earlier years, and to have shoplifted quite heavily when he was a teenager, and long before first taking Ecstasy.

Most, too, claimed never to have incurred debts because of their use of Ecstasy. Gael, however, a 20 year old employee who is a light stable user of Ecstasy, commented:

"At the moment, I don't manage ... well, I've never taken beyond ... this is [about] when I first started, but I wouldn't do this now ... I took £50 out of my bank account because I wanted to go to this rave ... I sold a camera so that I could go to a rave, and my pal lent me £100 ... .I would have been, 18,19 then ... Em ... now I don't take E ... not very often ... once every couple of months ... em ... because I'm on the dole again, so at the moment, I just can afford it. I still owe £270, but that's not all for E. About £100 of that is for E but ... em ... he said, 'Just give it me whenever' ... because he's got a job, and he makes 2 grand a week ..."

Much more typical was to reassert the relatively elastic nature of Ecstasy as a purchase. Iain, one of the medium erratic users (a 20 year old employee) claimed:

"Well, I'm working, and I've got quite a good job ... erm ... I get a reasonable wage for it, and if I've got no money, I don't do E. If I can't afford it, I don't go out. It's as simple as that. It doesn't bother me. I like to go out, but it's ... I just go somewhere else rather than go to the dancing ..."

And, in any case, as this 27 year old employee (Fiona, a heavy stable Ecstasy user) wryly commented, buying Ecstasy can also be an exchanged purchase, even amounting to net savings rather than net losses. When asked whether or not buying Ecstasy affected her financially:

"No ... I would say I'd probably spend more on drink if I was on the bevvy. Well, I would spend the same. Ever since I was fifteen, I've been going to night clubs, so that's always been part of my budget ..."

BINGEING

As with other stimulants, some Ecstasy users "binge" sometimes. This has two meanings. First, "stacking" (i.e., taking several tablets at once). Second, "boosting" (i.e., taking several tablets but at intervals over a period of time such as an evening, or several days). During a binge users may both stack and boost.

Bingeing on Ecstasy

Looking first at information provided by the large sample, the data don't permit a distinction to be made between those claiming to have binged, but who were boosters, who were stackers, and/or who were both. Eighty-one users reported bingeing at least once and of them, 46 reported bingeing more than once, but only 15% of bingers had binged on more than 10 occasions, with one respondent reporting 98 binges. For comparison purposes, bingers who had binged once were compared to those who had binged at least twice.

Thirteen users had taken 2.5 or fewer tablets during their last binge (people took as little as a quarter tablet at a time). Another 13 had taken 3–3.5 tablets, 19 had taken 4–5.5 tablets, 19 6–9 tablets and 17 9.5–100 tablets. Another way of considering these data is to average the number of tablets taken by the number of days that the binge lasted. Those whose binge had lasted a day or less had taken on average 2.6 tablets, while those whose binge lasted two or more days had taken about the same number of tablets a day. This suggests that boosting was more substantial in this group than stacking. This is supported by data on the number of tablets respondents reported using on the last occasion that they used Ecstasy. Seventy two percent reported consuming one tablet or less, 18% had used more than one, but not more than two tablets, 8% had used between 2 and 3 tablets, leaving only 2% who had used more than three but no more than five tablets.

Most users who binged, binged for less than four days, although one person had binged for 21 days. A quarter of those who had binged had binged for two days, with 14% claiming to have only binged for a day. It isn't easy to tell what bingeing for "one day" means, as this could cover any period from a few to 24 hours. However, we can fairly assume that those who responded to the questions on bingeing (and were not given a definition of a binge) found that it meant something to them, perhaps much in the same way as most cocaine users interviewed in our earlier study seemed to know what a "heaviest period" of cocaine use was.

Users differed in terms of how many binges they claimed to have been on. Table 2.2 shows how this varies by user group. Generally, considering first the italicised summary rows, the more extensive the use of Ecstasy, the more binges the user had been on. For example, 76 per cent of the heavy users have binged at least once (and a majority of them have binged two or more times), whereas only 16 per cent of the light users have binged at all (half of them only once). Within each use level, erratic users were more likely to have binged at all, and were more likely to have binged more than once.

Table 2.2 also shows, for each group, how long, in days, their last binge lasted. Generally, again considering the italicised summary rows (and recognising that this data only relates to the last binge the respondent had been on), the more extensive the use of Ecstasy, the more likely that users had been on longer binges. For example, only 7% of all light users had binged for more than 5 days the last time they binged, but this rises to 14% of the medium users, and to 27% of the heavy users. There is no obvious relationship between stability of use, and length of last binge and there were no significant effects of group or pattern on length of binge.

BINGE FREQUENCY AND DURATION BY USER GROUP

GROUP	Users that had binged only once	Users that had binged more than twice	Bingers whose last binge lasted 1–2 days	Bingers whose last binge lasted 3–4 days	Bingers whose last binge lasted 5–21 days	Bingers who would binge again
(n)	%	%	%	%	%	%
Ex-users	11	–	–	67	33	–
Light stable	10	7	57	29	14	17
Light erratic	7	10	57	43	–	33
ALL LIGHT (14)	*8*	*8*	*57*	*36*	*7*	*16*
Medium stable	4	16	60	40	–	40
Medium erratic	23	29	38	46	17	57
ALL MEDIUM (30)	*16*	*25*	*41*	*45*	*14*	*38*
Heavy stable	30	39	25	38	38	50
Heavy erratic	27	55	39	44	17	77
ALL HEAVY (34)	*29*	*47*	*32*	*41*	*27*	*42*
ALL (81)	15	20	39	43	19	51

Table 2.2

ECSTASY CONSUMPTION DURING LAST BINGE FOR THOSE WHO HAD BINGED EVER IN DAYS, BY USER GROUP					
GROUP	1–2.5	3–3.5	4–5.5	6–9	9.5+
(n)	%	%	%	%	%
Ex-users	–	–	–	67	33
Light stable	14	29	14	29	14
Light erratic	29	43	29	–	–
ALL LIGHT (14)	*21*	*36*	*21*	*14*	*7*
Medium stable	20	40	20	20	–
Medium erratic	24	20	16	20	20
ALL MEDIUM (30)	*23*	*23*	*17*	*20*	*17*
Heavy stable	13	–	25	6	56
Heavy erratic	6	6	39	44	6
ALL HEAVY (34)	*9*	*3*	*32*	*27*	*29*
ALL (81)	**16**	**16**	**24**	**24**	**21**

Table 2.3

Table 2.3 shows how many Ecstasy tablets were consumed during the last binge. Again (and again ignoring the ex-users, the light users and the medium stable users, of whom there are too few to support any further analysis) the trend was for the number of Ecstasy tablets taken during the last Ecstasy binge to be greater for heavy than for medium users, and for erratic than for stable heavy users.

Combining with Other Drugs

Table 2.4 shows the other drugs taken during Ecstasy binges. All drugs reported as taken by at least 2 respondents are included. Several observations can be made about this data. First, very few bingers (8% – 6 of the 80) binge on Ecstasy alone, and these are more likely to be medium or heavy users. Second, other than this, the data seems to support the idea that people have "binges" rather than are "bingers". When bingeing, users typically use more than just Ecstasy. Overall, cannabis and amphetamines were the most popular other drugs, closely followed by hallucinogens (if psilocybin use is added to LSD use).

Nearly two fifths also use alcohol, a quarter or fewer use cocaine and temazepam, and just two used heroin. Overall, there is clearly a preference for co-use of hallucinogens and stimulants. Temazepam and heroin may have been used at the end of the binge, to assist come-down, but no specific questions were asked about this. Finally, looking at the average number of drugs used, there are only enough

OTHER DRUGS TAKEN DURING LAST ECSTASY BINGE

	ex-users	light stable	light erratic	medium stable	medium erratic	heavy stable	heavy erratic	ALL
n =	3	7	7	5	25	16	18	81
% No other drug	–	–	–	20	16	6	–	7
% Alcohol	67	43	71	40	25	44	33	38
% Cannabis	67	43	71	60	46	44	61	52
% Amphetamines	–	57	43	40	56	50	61	52
% Psilocybin	–	14	14	40	–	–	–	5
% LSD	33	43	43	60	56	31	39	44
% Cocaine	33	14	29	60	17	25	28	25
% Temazepam	–	14	–	–	13	25	11	12
% Heroin	–	–	–	20	–	–	6	3
% **Average no. of drugs in binge**	2.0	2.4	2.7	3.4	2.2	2.3	2.5	2.4

Table 2.4

respondents in the medium erratic, heavy stable and heavy erratic categories to support any analysis, and here it can be seen that the average number of other drugs used progressively increases.

Would they binge again? Data is in the right hand column of Table 2.2. Again, preparedness to binge again is related both to frequency of use and to stability of use, with heavy users being more likely than medium users to say so (and medium users, in turn, more likely than light users); and with erratic users in each of the three use groups being more prepared than stable users to binge again.

What does "bingeing" mean? Turning now to the small group, 18 of the 22 responded to a question on whether or not they had "ever been on an Ecstasy binge", and 10 responded firmly that they never had. Sharon, however, a light erratic user, admitted that, "*bingeing was certainly my style with alcohol, but not with E*", and Phil, a 19 year old employee who was a heavy erratic user, had trouble distinguishing binge use from normal (for him) use:

"*...eh? ... I have, but it's not really a binge. I get full of it on the Friday night, say full of Eccy, then take a drink during the day, and then I take more Eccy and other drugs. So that's Friday night, and all day Saturday, Saturday night, and then Sunday up to the afternoon, and I end up falling asleep. That's my usual weekend. It's not really a binge ...*"

These interpretative difficulties are compounded for those who do confess to bingeing. For example, a binge for a light user is nothing more than normal use for a heavy user. For example, one light stable user (Naomi, a 23 year old employee) took a half tablet on two consecutive nights, and referred to it as a "binge". Another light stable user, this time Stuart, the 28 year old student, took two whole tablets on each of two consecutive nights. He recalled:

"Aye, those lemon and limes, I had two on a Friday night, and then another two on the Saturday night. I suppose that was a bit of a binge, but they were quite pure ... I was a bit shattered, as if your time clock had been fucked, you know ... but nothing major. An E binge is good. It clears out the cobwebs. It just exhausts your mind and body. Och! That's a drug addict's excuse! 'Clear the cobwebs out!' ... Aye, it's just a binge. It shatters you. You need a good week to recover, just staying watching TV or just chilling out, you know ..."

Four of the five light erratic Ecstasy users had never binged: the one who had (Richie, a 30 year old employee) remembered:

"With Ecstasy, I just like the notion of staggering Ecstasy, but that's not all the time ... the biggest binge was in my house when I took 4 or 5 within the space of two, two and a bit days. That's not excessive, I guess, but I just kept taking it at regular intervals ... kept up there for a couple of days. It was very nice. I was in good company, people I liked. I was in my own home, apart from anything else, had a nice party, loads of people around. It was good fun, nothing untoward happened. We eventually sort of coasted down a couple of days later, went to the pub, had a few beers, just went home ... That kind of stuff's fine once in a while, wouldn't make a habit of it. If that's your regular weekend, you know, personally I don't think that's terribly healthy. I think that actually could become quite boring. Very routine after a while ... but a binge, as you say, which is a great word, yeah, it was great. Good fun. No problems resulting from it ... well ... fatigue and tiredness. Had to take a day off. Probably took a day of work actually, but that's alright because I've got the sort of job where I can put in the extra hours at some other time ... nobody else was at risk. I wasn't being irresponsible in that sense ..."

The two medium stable users who responded both denied having ever binged; yet the two medium erratic users both confessed to having done so. The first (Liz, a 19 year old employee) was less sure. She reported:

"...it depends what you mean by a binge. I mean I've never taken more than one and a half Eees at one time, and I suppose the only time I've done it is that weekend in Manchester ... It probably was a binge, actually, if I think about it. I probably took 4 ... em ... we went down on the Friday night, and we were actually in Liverpool, and it was an all-night thing, so we took a half at the beginning of the night and then about 3 or 4 o'clock, we took, I think we took another one, and then at a party that morning, we took another half and went to bed. Then back to Liverpool, took another one, went back to the party in Manchester, took another one, went to a club in the morning, took another half, and that was it ... Started on the Friday night, and finished on the Sunday day ... So I suppose that's the only time I've ever done that ..."

Iain, the other medium erratic user (a 20 year old employee) was sure that he had binged on at least one occasion:

"One day, at New Year, there was a party at my house, and I swallowed 8 throughout the whole night from Saturday night from about 8 o'clock through until about Sunday night at about 3 o'clock in the morning ... Over the space of 18 hours, I swallowed 8 or 9. One every two hours ... em ... basically, it was a good party, even if I say so myself ... that's the longest I have ever done if for, but that was just a once off ... [afterwards, I felt] ... like shit ... Yes, em, it was the next day. I'd actually got to sleep on the Sunday at 3 o'clock in the morning, woke up on Monday after about 8 hours sleep, but I didn't feel too good, but I wasn't actually feeling too bad considering actually what I'd taken. I took about a quarter of an ounce of sulph[19], brought out a carving board, and drew out some lines and said, 'Right! Everyone just help yourselves'. I took some and cleaned up the house, and went down to my pal's house that night as I didn't have any money. I just took half an E, and that was it. It was fine. I was back to normal after that had worn off. Tuesday, I felt fine. I got a good night's sleep, and felt fine. Tiredness, more than anything. Lack of sleep. It catches up with you no matter how long you go on a binge. It catches up on you eventually, no matter how much you take ..."

The heavy Ecstasy users have trouble distinguishing binge use from what is, or was, for them normal use. As one heavy stable user (Fiona, the 27 year old employee) put it, bingeing can be either stacking or boosting:

"I tend to do binges, and then come off it. It's always at the weekend, though. It's never during the week ... Well, it's not that much of a binge. It's just like, 3 or 4 maybe, over a weekend, and then I'm back down to one. ... I tend to do a half every hour, and then I can stay at that plane. So if I'm doing that, that's alright. Saturday there, I took two in a whack. I just did the both of them, so I didn't do it [binge] then ... .but that's not what I'd normally do. It's normally every hour. The last time I took 4, I must have gone in at about 12, and I'd have taken a half then, and then a half, yeah, a half every hour until about 8 ..."

The other heavy stable user, 19 year old unemployed Moira, also claimed to boost in the same way (a half every hour), but only to have done so once. The one heavy erratic user who responded to this question, Willie, a 24 year old unemployed man, binged regularly at one point in his past, something he could then afford to do as he was selling Ecstasy as well as using it:

"...4 or 5 days in a row. I don't know. I was doing a lot of E ... em ... up until a year and a half ago. I was doing a lot of E every weekend, and it would be about Friday, Saturday and Sunday, you know, peter-ing out towards the Sunday. Going to the clubs on the Friday, and then just carrying it right through to the Sunday. On the Friday, it would be two, two and a half Eees, and acid. Then on Saturday, have maybe one, one and a half Eees, and then winding down, and then on Sunday, just having half of one, or three quarters, or something, and some malt whisky ... I would have been taking other drugs at the time, and if I had cocaine, I would have taken it so ... a bit of cocaine the next day, and some valium the next day, some uppers and downers ..."

The one ex-user (Charlie, a 22 year old unemployed man) was the only one to report what might be seen as dangerous bingeing:

"Binge? ... yeah. In 1992, I took 48 Phase Fours over a period of 4 days. Just me. I got out of control of myself ... I went through it all myself, and rode it all out. Locked myself in the house. Couldn't eat. Couldn't sleep. I never slept for, like, 14 days. Couldn't eat. All I was doing was drinking cold soup, and drinking Milk of Magnesia ... my body was getting screwed, and I was like getting shakes, and stuff like that ... I never injected it. But I smoked it, snorted it, ate it ... It took me 14 days to come out of it. There wasn't a lot of mind symptoms

then. Most of it was body. Most of it was my physical body vomiting, diarrhoea, sweats, and feeling very cold. This was like after I ran out of E ..."

Soon after, he gave up using Ecstasy altogether.

We will look more closely at giving up Ecstasy later, in Chapter Four. In the next chapter, we consider more specifically the actual use of Ecstasy. To what degree do the fabled set and setting play in the Ecstasy experience? What truth is there in the much-touted idea that it is an aphrodisiac? And, more gloomily, what does it feel like when the effects of Ecstasy wear off?

NOTES

[17]   Easterhouse is one of Glasgow's notorious peripheral housing schemes, built during the 1950s and subject to poverty and deprivation since. Although it has been somewhat improved in recent years, this respondent is using "from Easterhouse" more-or-less as a polite synonym for "ned".

[18]   When someone goes very pale and feels sick – often after smoking cannabis.

[19]   Amphetamine Sulphate – powder form, often called speed.

CHAPTER THREE
Uses of Ecstasy

Perhaps because of the success of its initial marketing, Ecstasy rapidly gained a reputation as something of an aphrodisiac – even to the extent of being dubbed "the love drug" in the British media. Aficionados later detected an ambiguous effect in this respect, and the love drug thereafter became "the hug drug". What did members of our small group think of combining Ecstasy use with sex?

"Yeah ... you're much more sensitive to someone touching you, and you basically feel as if you're orgasming all the way through it, and then if you have an orgasm, you go onto this level never experienced before..." (Gael)

"...it enhanced it, definitely. Em ... you just let go an awful lot more, and, like, your sense of touch and everything ... everything is exaggerated..." (Morag)

"Aye! ... it makes it a lot better! ... I don't know. You just feel really horned up. You're like, 'Here! You!' ... Grab! It's just like you love folk more: you fancy folk more..." (Moira)

"Men seem to say that it's better, even better for them. To put it bluntly, they find that they can have sex for a lot longer on Ecstasy ... em ... a lot longer..." (Liz)

"Aye. It ... enhances your performance ... just like staying power for the guy..." (Stuart)

"It's like everything's in slow motion with E. I'd say it was quite good. Aye, it's different..." (Agnes)

THE RIGHT MOOD AND THE RIGHT PLACE

The Right Mood

Most of the small group seemed to believe that Ecstasy use is suggested by social circumstances, rather than by individual mood. That doesn't mean to say that Ecstasy doesn't have an effect on mood: instead, that one doesn't have to be in a particular mood to benefit from it. Ecstasy is believed, by some, to help with "bad" moods. Sometimes this is thought to depend on the type of Ecstasy to hand, as with this 23 year old employed woman who is a light stable Ecstasy user. Naomi told us:

"I think ... em ... if I'm in a bad mood, I would choose to take it to get me out of the bad mood, and sometimes it works, and sometimes it doesn't ... Depends on what kind of E you get. I know that I enjoy ones that are ... if they're light and they make me dance, I'll forget what I was bothered about, and I'll get up and dance. I think ... eh ... it probably does make me forget what I was depressed about, but it doesn't stop me being depressed ... if I'm in a bad mood, I tend, I think, not to take E actually. I will usually decide against it. You know what I mean. But if I do, it's usually, 'Oh, to hell with it! I'll just do it!' ... you know, 'Let's take some!' ... and if it's sort of speedy, then, yeah, it'll really improve my mood, but if it's not, and it's a bit heavy or whatever, it probably makes it worse ..."

The best attainable, then, is temporary relief if the "right" type of Ecstasy is available. As Danny, a light erratic user (and a 21 year old employee) put it, *"I reckon if you're ratty before you take it ... then the next morning when you wake up, you are just going to be as ratty as before"*. However, for others, the prospect of some Ecstasy, and associated delights, can itself brighten up horizons (Kirsty, a 20 year old student, who was a light stable Ecstasy user commented that she felt: *"...yeah, always just kind of excited about going out, and what the night might hold for you, it's quite exciting ..."*). For still others, even if the relief from temporary depression is itself temporary, a net gain occurs. Fraser, a 43 year old employee who is now a light erratic user put it like this:

"Although there have been times when ... eh ... when I've been fairly down, and I've taken E, where it has cut through all of that, and the initial stages of taking E ... no matter what was going on in my life ...

eh … how harassed, or whatever else … If I was out, and I was taking E, everything else would go out of the window, and I would just party and have a good time, and the rest of it …"

None said that using Ecstasy put them in a bad mood, and most that it helped with temporary depressions of various sorts, as well as perking people up at the end of a tiring work week in ways that alcohol does not. This is Morag, a 22 year old employee who is a medium stable Ecstasy user:

"…when I've worked hard … I used to, like, have a really busy week at work, or whatever, and you are shattered and you just want to go out and enjoy yourself and you felt that you had to take something to give you that extra Umph! to get you out and be happy, because if I went out and I was straight, and had a couple of drinks, of whatever, I'd sit and fall asleep in the corner …"

One person summed it up. Phil, a 19 year old employee who is a heavy erratic Ecstasy user. If you are down, Ecstasy will take you up: if you are up already, you'll just feel the same:

"Sometimes, usually if you don't want to go out somewhere, and you don't want to go out, and you don't want to swallow E … If you do swallow E, you have a great time. But if you do want to go out some-where, and you're really looking forward to it, and you take E, you're like, 'Is this it?' … That happens quite a lot … not if you're dead happy, but it's usually a kind of Sod's Law … if you want to go out and enjoy yourself, you'll end up having an alright night. But if you think, 'Oh, I cannae afford to do this', or 'I don't want to do this and I don't want to do that' … you go out and you end up having a great time. If you are on a downer, and you take Eccy, it cheers you up because it makes you feel better, because you think, 'Oh, I feel great now!'. But if you're already happy, and you take something that makes you feel happy, it just makes you feel the same …"

The Hazards of Buying

Being in the mood is one thing: drugs still have to be obtained, and Ecstasy is a Class A drug with all the attendant dangers that buying in that class entails. The light users were far more wary of this, and also, being less experienced, more wary about being sold imposter substances, and tended not to buy in clubs. For some, as with this 20 year old employee, the danger is physical rather than legal. Gael:

"I would rather not buy it in a club. I would rather just try and get if off someone I knew because if you're going to score a dove … I remember quite a few times people trying to sell me paracetamol. You know, they seem a bit wary … This guy's like that, 'There you go!', and I was like that, 'Can I get a look?' … and he showed me, and I was like that, 'No, you're alright' … and you're walking away going, 'Is this guy going to thump me or something?' … you know what I mean? …"

Other light users are wary of buying because they might not only be caught, but be caught buying for friends. Stuart, the 28 year old student:

"I've never bought E in clubs, because, like, the DS [drug squad] might be might be mingling, or you might be buying it off the DS. I know people who have bought them in clubs and got, like, OK stuff. And I know people who have bought it in clubs, and got, like, DFs or something, and paid 15 … 20 quid for them. But I don't want to know the dealers, because if you start getting to know people, it's just too easy to get Eees, and then you start getting them for other people, and then, like, you've got like 10 Eees or something like that on you, and then you're banged away for 5 years … It's not such a cool drug, like coke. Know what I mean? If you're getting coke, the people are really paranoid and cool about it. If you get Eees, the people are a bit more neddy and not West Endy, and might say stupid things over the phone, and drop you in it, you know … I deal indirectly with people. If somebody's getting Es, then I'll order one with them …"

These light users also preferred to take their Ecstasy before entering a club to further reduce the risks of apprehension. The medium level users bought both before entering, and whilst inside clubs. As distinct from the light users, the medium users seemed to know how to buy unproblematically, although, as in this case (Iain, a 20 year old employee) this doesn't guarantee quality:

"I usually try and get hold of it before I go. In a club, it tends to be one sort of gang in a club that does the dealing. Everybody knows them, but you only get the main person, if you know who that is. It's the quiet one in the corner who will deal without anyone else knowing.

You see who's hanging about, and then you're in ... [what you get] ... depends on your luck. I mean, you can be going to the same person for weeks, and then, just like that, the stuff's no good. It just depends on the batch that he gets in, what he gets. There was one time, I got mine before I got in, and I got good ones. My pal bought his when he got in, and he didn't get a hit off his at all. It just depends on your luck ..."

Heavy users buy both outside clubs and in, but express no prospective difficulty in finding a dealer even in a strange club. As Kath, a 25 year old employee who was a heavy stable user commented:

"Yeah ... I could probably ... you can spot a dealer after you've been using it for a while ... It's just what they're doing. You can spot a runner anyway: you can spot who's there and what's going on ..."

Moira (a 19 year old unemployed heavy stable user) replied, when asked how easy it was to buy Ecstasy in clubs:

"...dead easy. You can ask around. I usually get mine before I go in, but I've bought in clubs on occasion. There's always a pal that knows a pal that knows someone that you know ..."

For other heavy users, being sold imposter substances poses no irresolvable problems. Willie, a 24 year old unemployed man who was a heavy user (and also a sometime dealer) put it like this:

"Yeah ... dead easy [to buy in clubs] ... maybe not to guarantee what you're going to get, but if you're not prepared to be done over by anyone ... like if I got a duff E, I be like right back to the guy that sold it me, and I'd be like, 'Money? I've got a problem' ... unless it's a club where the bouncers are in control, you're going to get your money back, and you're going to get another one somewhere else ..."

The Need for Sociability

Irrespective of where it is bought, consumption of Ecstasy seems primarily to be a social rather than an individual affair. Of all those interviewed, only a few of the erratic users admitted that they had taken Ecstasy alone. Richie, a 30 year old employee (and a light erratic user) claimed that he had taken Ecstasy when alone *"or I'm by myself after taking E. I've no particular preference ... I don't go out seeking* company. I'm not particularly inclined to shut people out, I just depends what's happening at the time ... doesn't bother me", and another (Fraser, the 43 year old employee who was also a light erratic user) claimed to prefer company, but did not rule out solitary use:

"It's more of a ... it's the people ... it's more the event that make it, you know ... but I have, on occasion, sat in and taken an E, and maybe watched a movie at home ... because it was there, because I had it, because I didn't want to ... particularly want to go out, and fancied getting high, and I thought, 'I'll just do that, you know?' ... that was OK ... yes, with certain movies it did give me ... it does heighten empathy, there is no doubt about it ... there's one particular movie, it had a huge effect on my. ... 'Ordinary People', it was ... I remember watching that and I was high on E, and really got drawn into the emotions of it, so ... yeah ... it kind of opens you up that way ..."

But for the rest, the closest to solitary consumption came from Willie again, a 24 year old unemployed man who was a heavy erratic user, who mentioned that he had, "...popped bits of E just when I was going out ... not knowing if I was going clubbing or anything, and that was fine ...". Some, indeed, had never even thought of taking Ecstasy alone. As Euan, a 27 year old employee who was a light erratic user put it, "no, I wouldn't want to ... I don't see the point in that ... I've never had the opportunity to do it, and I wouldn't say it was something I would make time to do ...". Similarly, Fiona, a 27 year old employee who was a heavy stable Ecstasy user told us:

"I've never really thought of it ... I'm never really much on my own ... eh ... I've never really thought about taking it on my own, as I say, it's a social thing, never thought about staying in and taking an E ..."

Looking, briefly, at the large sample, it is possible to make some sort of assessment of how "sociable" these Ecstasy users are. There, each was asked how many close friends they had in the area where they lived, how many of them went to dance clubs, how many of them went to raves, how many of them used Ecstasy, how many of them had problems with it, and how many of them sold Ecstasy. The large sample claimed to have an average of 7 friends each, and 95% of the 1526 close friends claimed (by the 217 members of the sample that answered that question) went to dance clubs, and 59% to raves. They estimated that 92% of them used Ecstasy, that 7% of them sold Ecstasy, and that 5% had problems associated with using it. Those with a stable use pattern were more likely (understandably) to have friends who sell Ecstasy, otherwise there was no relationship between these variables and the levels and patterns of respondents' Ecstasy use.

The remainder of the small group positively reserved Ecstasy for occasions when others were present, and when they, themselves, were out. As one put it, Ecstasy is *"really to go out on"*, or as Kirsty, a 20 year old student who was a light stable user reported, using alone, *"doesn't really appeal to me. It's a ... it's a 'have a laugh' type of thing that I like. I would prefer to do it with friends. I mean ... I'm not ... It's doesn't really interest me, doing it on my own"*.

Being in the Right Place

Two other reasons were advanced for not consuming Ecstasy alone. First, expressed by Naomi, a 23 year old employee who is a light stable user:

"Because it's usually ... a lot of the time I don't think about taking it until I'm out at a club ... em ... I never usually buy it in any other environment, and when I buy it, I take it then and there ... I don't usually have any to take [anywhere else] ... a lot of the time, if I'm not in a ... I don't mean if I'm not in a great mood ... but I'm not really lively, and I want to have a great night ... that's the reason I take it ... So I wouldn't sit in by myself and take it ... definitely not ..."

Second, a more practical point, this time from Iain, a 20 year old employee who was a medium erratic Ecstasy user:

"I usually only take it if I'm going to the dancing, or to a party. I'd rather be full of it with someone else there. I always do it with my friends, whether they're taking it or not. I'll take it myself, but I've never taken it being by myself. I like to talk. No matter how daft you are ... whether you can talk or not ... you like to mumble to someone whether they can understand you or not, it makes you feel not isolated. I don't like to feel isolated: start to get paranoid ..."

Simply being out (and with others) is enough for some (*"if you're comfortable with yourself and with your pals, then I don't really see why there should be a problem anywhere"* from Kirsty, a 20 year old student who was a light stable user), but most specified other conditions. For a few, the others either have to be using Ecstasy at the same time (*"aye, it's best to take them in a place where everybody else is on them ... on the same wave length"* from Moira, a 19 year old unemployed heavy stable user), or at least to be aware of drug use and the likely effects. As Phil, a 19 year old employee who was a heavy erratic user put it, it isn't good to take Ecstasy:

"...around anyone who is not into the same thing ... or a place where there is no one else who is into drugs, and no one else knows anything about the drugs, or understands anything about them ... they make you feel ... you feel very uneasy ..."

Two more felt the same way. First, Fraser, the 43 year old employee who was a light erratic user; and second, Iain, a 20 year old employee who was a medium erratic user:

"Eh? ... where not to take Ecstasy? ... obviously anywhere you'd feel threatened, you know, anywhere where you would feel uncomfortable, anywhere where you'd feel you might be in danger ..."

"It depends on the person. I don't like taking drugs when there's people about, say I'm in a party with just, like, 3 or 4 friends, and there's lots of folk there that I just don't know. I don't like to take any because you never know how they are going to react to the state you're in. They might take offence to the way you're acting. So that's why I don't like taking it, because I am a wee bit more self conscious of what you actually do. You don't tend to enjoy yourself as much because you don't know the people ... but when you go to the dancing, then everybody seems to ... everybody knows you going to be full of it ... everybody knows what you've taken, and if everybody knows you've taken something ... even the drinkers in there, the people that don't touch it, know you've taken drugs ..."

Outwith that sort of situation, drinkers – even pubs – are spurned. Naomi, a 23 year old employee who was a light stable user commented, *"I wouldn't really do it if I was going out to a pub: I would do it if I was going out for an evening out to a club"*, and Agnes, a 20 year old employee who was a medium stable user, expanded:

"I wouldn't take it in a pub. Pubs are a bit brighter, more open, and there's a lot of people just drinking in it. So, you're going to look more of an idiot with your eyes, and you can get sort of light-headed, and

you'd be paranoid. Maybe everyone else wouldn't notice you were on it, but I would be paranoid. End up going home ..."

CLUBBING AND RAVING

For most of the small group, then, taking Ecstasy means clubbing or raving. Is there any noticeable relationship between clubs and dancing in the large sample? All were asked if they had ever been to dance clubs, raves, illegal parties and DJ'd private parties, and if so, on how many days in the year prior to interview. All but one had been to a dance club, most (93%) to DJ'd private parties, and about two-thirds to raves (65%) and illegal parties (62%). Only a handful had only ever been to just one type of venues, 17% to two of them, 37% to three of them, and 43% to all four. Heavier users of Ecstasy tended to have been to more types of venue, but there was no relationship with pattern of use. Similarly with the number of days they had done so in the past year: overall, about 18% had done so on up to 26 days (up to fortnightly), 32% on between 27 and 52 days (fortnightly to weekly), 31% on 53 to 104 days (from weekly to twice weekly), and 19% on 105 days or more (more than twice a week). Stable or erratic pattern of use doesn't explain any of this, but the greater the level of use the more often they go to these events.

The Absence of Hassle

However, in discussions with members of the small group, when it comes to clubbing and raving, gender (rather than level or pattern of use) creates the main distinctions. The women interviewed here claim to be happier in clubs where Ecstasy is being consumed, but alcohol is not. What comes strongly through the transcripts is the sense of relief at being able to enjoy a night out without sexual or other aggression. First, Liz, a 24 year old employee who was a medium erratic user:

"...for me, I suppose, it's a very good atmosphere ... em ... sort of just sort of feeling that if it's a particularly good club, or whatever, you know a lot of people, you know, who go every week, and it's the same faces, and you get to know a lot of people ... It's like, em, a group of friends all having a good time. I don't know ... there is something ... very young sort of hedonistic atmosphere about it, and it's sort of bound up with lots of males and females sort of scantily clad, sweating together, high on drugs. I don't know. I think the sort of sex thing is

*part of it for me. While I'm single ... you meet members of the oppo-
site sex, ... it's a good way to meet people, because it's not difficult ...
and all the sort of barriers that there are in a pub* [are not there] *...*"

Making friends (rather than meeting possible lovers) was often clearly
rated as important, as by Moira, the 19 year old unemployed heavy
stable user:

*"The atmosphere ... It's dead like you can actually feel an atmosphere,
you know ... like it's almost as though you can see it ... it's great!
Everybody's like dead happy, and they're all out for just a good time.
Nobody's out to fight, and nobody's out to, like, cause arguments, or
anything like that ... it's like, go out, pop an Eccy, dance about all
night, go to a party and go home. You know, it's like folk coming up to
you, you've never met, saying, 'Oh, right! How are you doing?' ... and
you're like, 'Alright!' ... I mean I've made some of my good pals that
way ... [one man] ... I met at the dancing, and the lassie he's staying
with, like they're just pals but they share a flat, he met her at the
dancing. You know, you meet all your pals through raves and dancing
... you keep in touch with folk, you can get a wee social circle. I've got
pals in Arbroath, in Livingstone, and down south in Newcastle ... you
know, you've just met at raves ..."*

This was confirmed by Sharon, a 19 year old employee who was
a light erratic user. She claimed that at good clubs, she got *"less hassle"*
from men, and that, *"they'll speak to you, yeah, but they won't bother
trying to chat you up probably. You still get the odd people, but it's like
everything else, but just not as much. You can be quite relaxed. You won't
get any hassle and you won't get any fights off anyone ... or, no one can
be bothered to do any of that anyway."* Some women claimed to prefer
raves to clubs because of the usual absence of alcohol at the former, and
the consequent likely absence of any alcohol-fuelled problems. This
comment on raves is from Fiona, a 27 year old employee who was a
heavy stable Ecstasy user:

*"...you're on a dance floor and everyone's smiling. It's like a feeling of
unity and you're all on the same wave length, the same sort of tribal
feeling ... It's not like you're in a normal club, and most people have
been drinking, and guys are coming up to you, and they're all staring
at you, and pulling you onto the dance floor and being abusive ... Aye,
the way they look at you, you know all they've got on their mind is to*

getting their end away. Sorry! 'Having sex' with you! ... It's not like that in a rave. You'll be walking about, and guys will give you a cuddle, and they'll be, like, 'Oh, right!', shake your hand, and say, 'Where are you from?' and then they're like, 'Have a good night' and they just leave you alone ..."

But, she continued:

"...at raves, guys just want to be your sort of friend. There is definitely no sexual ulterior motive to it ... half the time at raves I wander about on my own, you know, I'd want to take off on my own, and I just wander about talking to loads of people. I really sort of knocked it on the head going to normal clubs after I discovered that ... you'd always bump into some pissed arsehole ... especially in Glasgow ... I'll always remember being with my friend at ... [a Glasgow club, where one man] ... he had a hold of her, and he was like pulling her onto the dance floor, but he'd a pint in his hand, and he was sloshing it everywhere, and he's like that, 'Fucking dance with me!' ... like, you would never get that at a rave ..."

This appears to be a rave scene which is passing, in favour of modern raves which are, according to Gael, a 20 year old employee who was a light stable Ecstasy user, *"full of 12 year old ravers"*. She added that many of the clubs have switched from house to techno music, and that, too, tends to attract younger people, and thus create a *"mad"* as opposed to a *"mellow"* experience. Finally, Naomi, a 23 year old employee, who was a light stable Ecstasy user, was even beginning to have doubts about the few remaining acceptable clubs:

"Up until recently, I would say that, from a female point of view ... I mean just going to the pub, there's like normal music and I suppose drunks and guys harassing you ... [but at the club] ... the guys on drugs, they are friendly, but that's it. But I would say that that's limited just now, due to the fact that there are a lot of not nice guys going there ... I think they're on Ecstasy, they're on something, anyway, they're not drunk ... I'm not sure whether it is the quality of the E, or the type of person now taking it. Clubs used to attract everyone ... it was quite happy. It was quite student, quite relaxed. Now, I go in and I look at people, and I think, 'Well, I'm not going to be able to communicate with them' ... they're quite frightening: quite neddish, quite aggressive ... girls as well ..."

The men, too, preferred the non-aggressive nature of the rave/club "culture" (although, contrary to what most of the women said, one did say that, *"if you want sex, it's the place to go"*). Stuart, a 28 year old student, who was a light stable Ecstasy users, typified most when he commented:

"Well, the thing about E is that you've got to take it at clubs where everybody else is taking them ... there's like a couple of hundred people on E, and it's just like a pretty mad experience. It's like all these adults going about and they're just like acting pure friendly towards each other. Nobody's going about chibbing[20] anybody: if you were all drinking, you would all be fighting. If you were all taking speed, you'd all be pure maniac. If you were taking mushies or acid, you'd all be mad. But when you're on E, you're all happy, and it's like hugging each other, and thinking, 'Wow! This is a good place to live' ..."

The Appropriate Music

Clubs – especially those playing house rather than techno music – were preferred, although many had complaints: *"it's extortionate that you've got to pay nine quid to get in"*, and *"queuing, you have to wait hours to get in"*, and *"a bottle of water that costs you £1.50 or £2"*, and *"the heat is tremendous"*, and (from Danny, a 21 year old employee who was a light erratic Ecstasy user):

"...it's dragging on a wee bit. Like, nothing's changed in about three years or something. The music's the same. It's still dance music, and it's still people taking the same drugs. It's just, like, the same thing. Nothing much has changed ..."

Nevertheless, all claimed to like the music independently of any association with clubs or with Ecstasy (*"I listen to that kind of music anyway"*, and *"I've got loads of rave tapes in the car and I drive all round the country, and I always listen to them"*). What Ecstasy adds to the generally sociable atmosphere is, in the words of Iain, the 20 year old employee who was a medium erratic Ecstasy user, is time and energy:

"...there have been occasions where I have been to the dancing, and I haven't taken anything, and I have enjoyed myself. Taking E keeps you up longer ... you haven't got the energy to dance for 5 hours solid, so

you take it, and if you start to feel tired, E just keeps you awake, keeps you going, and you just enjoy it longer ..."

Of, from Stuart, a 28 year old student who is a light stable user of Ecstasy:

"No you don't ... [need to take Ecstasy] ... because it's a hypnotic type of music, so you don't need to. But if you have taken E before ... then the E ... the feeling is like if you are in love with somebody, and there was a particular song about at the time ... and you hear it a few years later, and you feel good ... it's the same with E ... you can listen to rave music and you can really enjoy it ... your hands can feel silky, and your feet can feel good, and you start feeling good ..."

SEXSTASY

We have already referred to the rather chequered career of Ecstasy's relationship to sexual activity. We asked about it explicitly. Members of the large sample were asked four identical questions about sex under the influence of Ecstasy, and sex under the influence of alcohol: have you had sex when under the influence? With how many partners in the last year? How many of them were casual partners? And, how many of them did you always use a condom with? Their answers are summarised in Table 3.1.

Looking at Table 3.1, it can been seen that, first, more (89%) have had sex while under the influence of alcohol than have had it while under the influence of Ecstasy (64%); second, far more have had casual sex in the year prior to interview while under the influence of alcohol

SEX ON ECSTASY AND ON ALCOHOL								
	ex-users	light stable	light erratic	medium stable	medium erratic	heavy stable	heavy erratic	**ALL**
n =	28	41	42	25	48	23	22	**229**
% sex on Ecstasy	21	42	69	80	81	74	82	**64**
% casual sex on Ecstasy	11	17	26	40	33	35	41	**28**
% Ecstasy sex with condoms	20	36	62	50	45	50	53	**49**
% sex on alcohol	89	88	93	96	90	87	77	**89**
% casual sex on alcohol	36	59	50	44	52	48	23	**47**
% alcohol sex with % condoms	75	67	71	62	54	72	31	**61**

Table 3.1

(47%) than while under the influence of Ecstasy (28%); and, third, use of condoms "always" is more common – perhaps surprisingly – when having sex under the influence of alcohol (61%) than when under the influence of Ecstasy (49%).

"Love" or "Hug"?

What did the small group make of sex under the influence of Ecstasy? And did it make them more promiscuous? Here, gender is a more effective discriminator of opinion than is level of use. Those women who responded to this question (and more women did than did males) were most likely to say that Ecstasy increased the tactility and/or the "depth" of the experience. Here are two examples:

"Yeah ... you're much more sensitive to someone touching you, and you basically feel as if you're orgasming all the way through it, and then if you have an orgasm, you go onto this level never experienced before ... type of thing. But ... I've had a bit of a strange experience on E. When I was having sex, I kept falling asleep. I keep falling asleep on my boyfriend, and I was having these sort of wee sort of dreams ... but I thought they were actually happening. I was in the library ... and one minute I was shagging, and next I was in this library wandering about, looking at books ... and then my boyfriend woke me up and I went, 'Oh, have you seen that book?', and I just started talking as if ... you know ... that was a pretty strange night ..." (Gael, the 20 year old employee who is a light stable user).

"...it enhanced it, definitely. Em ... you just let go an awful lot more, and, like, your sense of touch and everything ... everything is exaggerated. It's much much better on E, but that's with my boyfriend. I would never ... like ... you would never take an E and grab the first guy because you felt horny. I wouldn't say it was like that. It just makes it feel better. I've only ever done it with somebody that I'm seeing, but that's me, right enough ..." (Morag, a 22 year old employee who is a medium stable user)

Another woman made almost precisely the opposite point. Moira is a 19 year old unemployed heavy stable Ecstasy user:

"Aye! ... it makes it a lot better! ... I don't know. You just feel really horned up. You're like, 'Here! You!' ... Grab! It's just like you love folk more: you fancy folk more. Don't know why. That's the one thing

about E that's not changed: you still feel that ... still feel that kind of 'Yeah! I want to rip the clothes off you' feeling ..."

For men, the effect was different, as even some of the women recognised. For example:

"I think ... em ... it makes you feel more tactile and just more ... you just feel more aware of your body. Men seem to say that it's better, even better for them. To put it bluntly, they find that they can have sex for a lot longer on Ecstasy ... em ... a lot longer ..." (Liz, a 19 year old employee who is a medium erratic user)

Men, in the main, agreed. Ecstasy increases both the length and frequency of sexual experience:

"Aye. It was quite good, actually. Aye. It just ... eh ... takes down sort of any barriers, you know like sort of inhibitions, and also enhances your performance ... just like staying power for the guy ... if sex feels like a good idea, it's a good idea, and it's as simple as that really. It's really good, and it's good the next day when you waken up, if you've actually gone to sleep. Having sex when you're drunk is crap, isn't it? ... the next morning on E, though, you'll probably feel like some more sex, because you've still, like, got the drug in your system ..." (Stuart, the 28 year old student who is a light stable user)

One woman, Agnes, agreed with this (albeit for different reasons). She is a 20 year old employee who is a medium stable user:

"Em ... it makes your body kind of numb, with E, normally. So, I'd say it takes you longer. If you weren't on drugs, you'd have an orgasm probably a lot quicker. It takes you longer. It's like everything's in slow motion with E. I'd say it was quite good. Aye, it's different ..."

A few respondents mentioned that the effect on sex varied with the type and quality of the Ecstasy being consumed. Two respondents – both women – found this:

"...again, it depends on what kind of Ecstasy you've taken. Sometimes it enhances it: sometimes you just don't even want to. You just want to lie in your bed and go to sleep ..." (Naomi, the 23 year old employee who is a light stable user)

"I wouldn't say it enhanced it, no. Not the actual sex. Probably the foreplay, and things like that. Probably by the time you got to that, you couldn't be bothered anyway ... You got that far, and then it is too much hassle to go on ..." (Sharon, the 19 year old employee who is a light erratic user)

The Ambiguity of Aphrodisia

Does Ecstasy make users more promiscuous? Of the eighteen that answered this question, only two said yes. Both men:

"I think E can make you ... definitely, for sure. I've got it together with people when I been Eeed up, and I probably wouldn't have got it together with them if I hadn't been taking E. Yeah, it's just because it makes you physical, and once you're raving and among friends, and no one minds hugging, and then if that feels good, and you tune into another person, then it just goes on from there. You know, so it's not so much that it actually makes you feel that you want to have sex with them ... but ... em it leads to physical ... because you want to touch and feel ... you go on from there ..." (Willie, the 24 year old unemployed heavy erratic user)

"Well, I was going to clubs more then, yeah ... I would shag anything ... but it depends what you are on ... you know, what kind of E ... with some, you just couldn't give a shit; and some E you were on, you'd be like that! Bloody hell! And it seems a lot better, but you don't remember the next day. Still, a shag's a shag, isn't it ? ..." (Danny, the 21 year old employee who is a light erratic user)

Most of the small group (10 of the 18) simply said "no". Their proclivity to promiscuity was unaltered either way by their use of Ecstasy, with one man even adding that he turned down more offers when using than at other times. Six volunteered the information that they were far more likely to have casual sexual relationships when under the influence of alcohol than when under the influence of Ecstasy. Here are some of their stories:

"...probably more with alcohol than E actually. On alcohol, you just don't give a shit, really. With E, you're dead touchy, you're dead cuddly, but that's as far as it goes. If anyone was to touch you somewhere, I would be like that! 'Oh, no' ..." (Morag, a 22 year old employee who is a medium stable user)

"...*with alcohol, you often end up with a guy of some sort, but E use has changed the perception of that. Now, because of E, I just can't be arsed going out with somebody that I know I would never really like in the long term ... Yeah ... For instance, if you're having a one-night stand on booze, then you're less aware of what you're doing. You generally don't give a shit about the guy you're sleeping with, and you probably feel a bit more hung up about it in the morning. But on E, you get to some level first with the person you're about to sleep with ... You feel some kind of closeness with them first ...*" (Kath, a 25 year old employee who is a heavy stable user)

"...*For example, if you were going clubbing, like drinking, like folk were just bevvied and that ... you would just go home at night ... but if you're taking Eees, you meet more people, and they're all friendly, so you might end up having a sexual relationship with them at the end of the night ... because you're both ... you're both wasted on E ... But you still know what you're doing ... but when you're drunk, you might think sex is a good idea, and you might say to the person, 'Yeah, sex is on the cards' ... and then you'll turn around a couple of minutes later, and they're steaming somewhere else, getting off with someone else ... When you're on E, you both kind of know what's happening. You're like that. 'Right, we're going to bed together, right?', and you say, 'Are we going home now? Let's stop off at the garage and get some condoms' ... but if you're steaming, you're like that! 'Whooooah! ... let's go the chippy and get some chips', get home at about 4 in the morning, and when you wake up, you're like that! 'Oh, my God. What a donkey!' ... and you're all smelly, and everything, you know? ...*" (Stuart, the 28 year old student who is a light stable user)

"I tend to have more casual relationships when I'm drunk ... there have been a lot of times when I could have had a casual encounter on Ecstasy, when I've said, 'No' ... sort of thing ...*" (Agnes, the 20 year old employee who is a medium stable user)

"*No, definitely not. I was more open to casual relationships before I started taking E. It's embarrassing when I think back on it, actually. Because of the things I used to do when I was pissed ... and a lot of the time, I didn't have ... when I was getting drunk all the time, I wouldn't even think of having protective sex ... Later, I met a boy that I had a relationship for two years with at a rave ... em ... but, like, I didn't go away with him the first night and have sex or anything like that ... but if I'd been steaming, I'd have been round the back, know what I mean?*

On E, you get more into people's minds, you're talking to people, and finding out about them. Whereas, when I was pissed, it was just, 'Haaaah!' ... when I was pissed, it was just, 'Let's have a shag' ..." (Fiona, the 27 year old employee who is a heavy stable user)

CHILLING OUT AND COMING DOWN

Chilling Out

Chilling out is resting temporarily from the fierce dancing that often accompanies Ecstasy use in clubs or at raves. Not everybody does it, but chilling out by clubbers isn't restricted to those that have consumed Ecstasy. Seventy per cent of the large sample said that there were chill out areas provided at the last dance event they attended, and of this sub-group of 160 users, only 24 (15%) had spent no time there chilling out. Most hadn't spent long there, and although the non Ecstasy using members of the sample were less likely to chill out, well over half of them had taken the opportunity to do so.

Because of the prospect of a harmful relationship between fierce dancing and dehydration from heat, the use of alcohol and/or the use of Ecstasy, the provision of chill out space and the availability of cool non-alcoholic drinks is of interest. Table 3.2 shows how much of what sorts of drinks were consumed by the large sample at the last dance event they attended.

From Table 3.2, it can be seen that three quarters of the large group drank alcohol (about a quarter of them quite heavily), almost three quarters drank no soft drinks, and over a third, no water. Rates don't vary significantly for different Ecstasy user groups, although (somewhat worryingly) the heavier the overall use of Ecstasy, the less likely are users to have drank water at the last dance

DRINKS CONSUMED AT LAST DANCE EVENT							
	ex-users	light stable	light erratic	medium stable	medium erratic	heavy stable	heavy erratic	**ALL**
n =	28	41	42	25	48	23	22	**229**
% no alcohol	36	12	24	16	23	48	41	**26**
% 9+ units of alcohol	14	29	26	24	19	22	36	**24**
% no soft drinks	64	81	71	80	64	61	59	**69**
% no water	50	44	33	36	33	26	27	**36**

Table 3.2

event they attended. Of course, the relatively availability and cost of water can be a problem. At the last dance event attended, 15% (34) claimed that water was free at the bar, 8% (18) that it was free at the bar and also available in the lavatories, 38% (88) that it was for sale in the bar, but also available free in the lavatories, and 20% (46) that it was available free in the lavatories. Of some concern, nearly a fifth of the sample said that water was either only available if bought at the bar (25 people, 11%), or, for 18 (8%) simply not available at all.

Feeling Unwell

A fairly large proportion (131, 58%) had felt unwell at some time or other at a dance event, and of this group, 30% hadn't taken any Ecstasy. However, 47% had taken a half or a whole tablet, and 23% had taken one and a half tablets or more. What else had they taken? Table 3.3 has the data.

The length of time that they felt unwell varied, but was not related to which Ecstasy using group they were in. The largest proportion of the 58% who had felt unwell at some time, felt unwell for less than 30 minutes (48, 38%), with 27 (22%) being so for between half an hour and an hour, 19 (15%) for one to two hours, and 31 (25) for longer than that. Table 3.4 collates the various symptoms claimed by those who had felt unwell, although it should be borne in mind that, when asked, two fifths of this group said that they had experienced similar symptoms at others times, and when they had not been at a dance event.

SUBSTANCES CONSUMED LAST TIME UNWELL AT A DANCE EVENT								
	ex-users	light stable	light erratic	medium stable	medium erratic	heavy stable	heavy erratic	**ALL**
n =	17	23	20	12	30	15	14	**131**
% Ecstasy	18	52	65	83	73	87	93	**70**
% alcohol	52	70	50	33	40	20	20	**43**
% cannabis	35	30	30	17	27	–	20	**24**
% amphetamines	6	26	35	8	30	20	33	**24**
% LSD	11	17	5	8	13	20	13	**13**
% cocaine	–	–	–	17	3	13	7	**5**
% poppers	6	4	–	8	–	–	–	**2**
% mushrooms	–	4	–	–	–	–	–	**1**

Table 3.3

	ex-users	light stable	light erratic	medium stable	medium erratic	heavy stable	heavy erratic	ALL
n =	16	22	19	12	30	15	14	128
% head	56	55	42	33	60	33	71	52
% stomach	18	23	32	42	33	40	14	29
% anxiety	31	18	26	8	23	20	36	23
% muscular	6	9	5	17	10	7	14	9
% psychosis	13	14	5	8	10	7	–	9
% disorientation	6	5	5	8	3	13	7	6
% breathing	18	–	–	8	7	–	–	5
% heart	–	5	–	–	–	–	–	1

SYMPTOMS EXPERIENCED LAST TIME UNWELL AT A DANCE EVENT

Table 3.4

What sort of help did they get when feeling unwell? Who provided it? Not much, and mostly from friends is the short answer. In rather more detail, 65 (50%) of the 131 answering this question claimed that they received no help at all. Of the other half of the unwell group, 32 (24%) just received general sympathy, 19 (15%) were given water, 6 (5%) were guided to fresh air, 4 got medical attention, with 5 specifying some other kind of help. Most of this help received by the 66 who received it was provided by friends, according to 48 (73% of the group), with 6 (9%) getting trained medical help, 3 (5%) assistance from club staff, and 9 (14%) from strangers.

Of these 131 people, on the last occasion they had been unwell 30% had not taken Ecstasy, 55% had taken 0.5–1 tablet and 23% had taken more than that (only 9% had taken more than 2 tablets). Some people had taken other drugs, with alcohol (43%), cannabis (24%) amphetamines (24%) and LSD (13%) being most common. Many people had felt unwell for 30 minutes or less (38%), although 25% had felt unwell for over two hours. The most common symptoms were "neurological" (51%) which involved things like feeling dizzy and "spaced out". Disorientation was also common (44%), as were gastric symptoms (39%) and anxiety (23%). Fewer reported muscular symptoms (9%) and less than 5% reported cardiac or respiratory symptoms.

In the small group there were as many attitudes to chilling out as there were interviewees. Some claim never to chill out at all ("*Well, I generally chill out by not going to them. When I go, I don't chill out at* all. No, I just fucking go for it, dance like a maniac", from Richie, a 30 year old employee who is a light erratic user).

Others reduce the speed, but not the fact of their dance pace. This from Stuart, a 28 year old student who is a light stable user:

"Well, a lot of people dance full-time non-stop, but what I do is I'll dance energetically, and then I'll just sort of slow down, dance sort of ambiently, and then maybe build up again, and then down, and then ... you regulate like a thermostat, like maybe on a half hour cycle, you know, something like that ..."

Others find it difficult to stop, most commonly because they have mixed amphetamines with Ecstasy. Sharon, a 19 year old employee who was a light erratic user commented: "again, it depends what you've taken. If you've taken more speed, you're likely to be up dancing more of the night", and Agnes, a 20 year old employee who was a medium stable user agreed: "With me, it depends. If I take speed with it, then I'll be dancing all night, but if I take it on it's own – I don't really like it on it's own – I end up sitting down most of the night ...".

A fairly common pattern is to intersperse periods of dancing with short periods of resting and drinking water (or cola: "sometimes you get sick of water"), with some occasionally having "a wee line of coke" to get them back in dancing mode. Some rest, but drink alcohol rather than water ("I don't drink water. I used to drink water, but now I just drink a beer, a gin and tonic ... just keep on drinking and drinking, and then a few cups of tea when I come home"), and some, as in the following case (Phil, a 19 year old employee who is a heavy erratic user), only at the end of the night, rather than periodically throughout it:

"...if I'm at a rave, I chill out for about two hours at the end ... you feel like ... you kind of stare up at the ceiling, and you go, 'Oh! Fucking great!' ... and then someone pours a bottle of water over you ... or else, if you just see them with sweat pouring off them, you offer them a drink of water to make sure they're OK ... I don't know why ... it's just a natural thing to do. A cup of tea's good as well. It's one of the best things. It's got lots of sugar in it ... you can get ice-cream and chips as well ..."

Coming Down

At some point, users come down from using Ecstasy. Whether or not other drugs are used to come down from Ecstasy use (and which ones) offers another way to discriminate between users. All four of the light stable users said that they used cannabis to come down, although none of the five light erratic users claimed to use anything stronger than, as one put it, *"hot cups of tea"*. All four medium users used cannabis to come down; the heavy stable users were more likely to use alcohol, and the heavy erratic ones, more likely to mention both heroin and temazepam.

The recalled nature of the come down also differed by type and level of use. Most of the light users either don't notice very much, or see the come down as relatively pleasant. As two of them put it (the first, Danny, a 21 year old; the second, Gael, the 20 year old):

"With E, it's quite quick, you know. Sometimes, you just snap out of it, you know. You're just like: 'Wow! Norm! Let's go home!' kinda thing … You don't really notice it. It's just, well, quite gradual, really. It's not a sudden kind of normal. You're not on E, anyway. You're kinda feeling normal, but not. Strange! You're clear … you're never … out of control …"

"My come downs off Eees, by themselves, are really, really nice. Yeah! You just feel quite fluffy and happy, and sort of quite contented to do anything. And the next day is sort of the same, you know. You … You can go for a walk in the park, you know, and you can sit and chill out. You don't get that sort of anxious, that you can get off speed. I mean, on speed come downs, you can get a bit narkey as well. You know what I mean? Sort of agitated, you know, get wound up really easily, and bite people's heads off and stuff if anything sort of pisses you off, and you're coming down off speed. But not on E … no …"

Other light users felt that dealing with an Ecstasy come down was a question of preparation: either before or after using Ecstasy itself. Two more, this time Stuart, a 28 year old student; and Naomi, a 23 year old employee:

"Sometimes you don't come down if it's good stuff. If it's like pure sort of E, and you haven't been taking them for a wee while, and you're healthy and, you know, you get a good sleep, and you just sort of look after yourself, and you eat breakfast and all that, and everything, and chill out. Go for a wee walk, and then there's no come down …"

"You can make it last a day, but occasionally it means going to the pub, having a few pints, quite nice, quite pleasant, fairly wasted and

wiped out by tea-time, and that's quite nice as well. You should be allowed days like that as long as it's not a work day, because it starts to get in the way then. That's also one of the big things about E, is that you can do it at the weekend, and fit it in with your lifestyle ..."

The light erratic users were not so content. One thought that come downs deteriorated with longevity of use career. As Sharon (a 19 year old employee) put it: *"I think when you first start taking it, it only lasts about a day. But I think the more you take it, the longer it [come down] lasts. It can take you until Wednesday, before you're alright. I think the longer you take it, the longer it takes before you're alright again. Definitely."* Another light erratic user (Fraser, a 43 year old employee who used to be a heavier user) thought that bad come downs were a result of excessive use:

"After taking it regularly for a period of two, three years ... three or four days after it, I would be hitting quite heavy depressions. Short-term, you know: irritable. You know, all the rest of it. And for quite a period, I was in denial: I would say that it was nothing to do with the E. But, gradually as time has gone on, I accept that yes, it was the E ..."

Medium level users (who have typically taken more other drugs, both during and after the Ecstasy experience) tend to mention general levels of tiredness both brought on, and alleviated by, use of other drugs; and seem relatively unable to distinguish the specific effects of Ecstasy. If at all, they tend to refer to a generic come down, which, given consumption of Ecstasy on a Friday or Saturday night, usually lasts until the early part of the next week. Heavier users appear to treat the experience as a repeating weekly cycle, as with this heavy stable user (Fiona, a 27 year old employee):

"Well, sometimes, I could go to sleep, but I don't want to ... I really enjoy the come down off of E. It's not like acid, and so you're not really disoriented and feel really weird. I like the come down off E: it's a really nice feeling. You feel really relaxed. I lie down in my bed at the end of the night, and it feels like I'm just sinking into the mattress: a really relaxing feeling. So, if I took an E on the Saturday, then on the Sunday, I would still have a bit of it in my system, and I feel quite relaxed. But, the real come down is on the Monday and the Tuesday, when you're back to reality, and you feel tired because you've been up all night, and sometimes I can be really snappy with my husband, and

you know, back to work and everything. But then, like, by the time it's Wednesday, I'm fine again. Tuesdays! Tuesday's the worst day. I think maybe on Monday, I'm still spaced from the weekend. Then on the Wednesday, I feel a bit better, and on the Thursday, better still, and on Friday, I feel really good, and then the weekend's there again ..."

The heavy erratic users (rather like the medium erratic ones) find it hard to distinguish which other drugs contribute to the come down, and which alleviate it. Here, Willie, a 24 year old unemployed male:

"Definitely, you need some sort of other drug if you've been up on three nights of E. You need valium or temazepam, or something, and anyway, you'll just be in your bed for the day, because you don't feel like going anywhere. If you were healthy and together, you could probably get up and jump about even after three days. But I'm not particularly healthy just now ..."

Most prefer to come down in the company of others, rather than alone. Only 3 of those interviewed (two light stable users, and one light erratic user) preferred to come down alone. One of the light stable users (Naomi, a 23 year old employee) put it like this:

"I prefer to do it on my own. I prefer to just go home to my bed, but a lot of the time you are with a group of people, and a lot of the time, we go somewhere. I like to go back to my flat, and just lie in my bed and relax and things. I quite enjoy that, actually. It's quite dreamy. You know, because a lot of the time, when you take drugs, it makes you quite heavy, it makes you feel quite lacking in energy, so it's quite good to sort of look forward to the come down. ... I lie, and I've got fish ... I lie and look at my fish. I might put some light music on, or whatever, but not a lot actually. Sometimes you drift in and out of sleep. Really, you dream a lot, but it's hard to tell whether or not you were actually asleep or whether you were sort of day dreaming. I do find it quite annoying, that way ... because a lot of the time I just want to go to sleep because after the club my body's tired, but my mind is sort of maybe a bit more awake, and I just want it to stop and just go to sleep ..."

Apart from the other two light users, all the remaining interviewees preferred to come down with others. Mostly, this was because they had tried coming down alone, but had not enjoyed the experience. As one light erratic user put it (Sharon, a 19 year old employee), *"if you are left on your own, you just become paranoid, and you can imagine things and get depressed, and your mind just runs away from you, basically*". One of the medium stable users (Sandra, a 24 year old employee) even went as far as ensuring that she never took Ecstasy alone because this would carry no guarantee that there would be others around for the come down. When asked if she had ever come down alone, she replied:

"Yeah ... it was bad. Your mind works overtime thinking hundreds of things. I don't know. It's kind of weird. For five minutes you might be alright ... be able to handle it ... you're in a daze, thinking about nothing, and the next minute you start freaking out, hearing noises as if they were there ..."

Others even indicated that the come down was part of the pleasure of Ecstasy – if, that is, it occurs in the company of others. Liz (a medium erratic user, and a 19 year old employee) compared the whole experience to drinking alcohol in groups:

"It's a very social thing ... I mean if I went out clubbing with 15 people and nobody else did it, then I don't think I would feel the same way about doing it ... I don't know ... there's this sort of conciseness among you all ... that you all feel the same way, ... which is different, say, from drinking ... There's no sort of mystery about drinking – do you know what I mean? But if it's a very happy E ... and you are with friends that you know well, and are close to, you are all feeling the same way, and are feeling happy ... it sort of intensifies the bond that you feel with them ... I mean, I have felt very happy when I've been drunk, but the happiness is different and the effects are different. Taking E you have this sort of unspoken thing which is just not there with the drink. If you've had an E, and feel really smacked, someone will say, 'Oh, I know how you feel', or, 'It's OK, I feel the same way too' ... it's the sort of thing you don't get with someone whose had ten vodka and cokes saying 'I feel the same way too' ..."

The heavy users were somewhat different. Some wanted to be alone to come down, as they were coming down from other drugs simultaneously, and, for example, as Willie (a 24 year old unemployed heavy erratic Ecstasy user) put it *"I like a bit of space when I'm coming down off it* [Ecstasy] *if I've taken acid as well"*, and other didn't want to be alone as there were still more drugs to be consumed during the come down, and this sometimes required collaboration. Another heavy erratic user (Phil, a 19 year old employee) put it like this:

"The routine is to go into a house and put music on, swallow a lot of drugs, have a smoke of hash, take some jellies ... you wait until the carry out shops [off-licences] *open, then you go down to the carry out at 8.00am, buy a big carry out, bring it up to the flat, and then you drink it, and then you usually fall asleep, and then you wake up with someone saying, 'it's time for you to go home' ..."*

It is probably easy to see now why we had such trouble finding people who consumed Ecstasy but no other drugs! We try, in the next chapter, to put Ecstasy use itself into some sort of context, critically by seeing what role Ecstasy plays in people's overall pattern of drug consumption, and how important our interviewees feel Ecstasy is in contributing to their overall lifestyle.

NOTES

[20]   Slashing with a razor, these days more likely a craft knife, or any indeed any attack with a blade.

Chapter Four
The Role of Ecstasy

Due to what we think is flawed questionnaire design, people who use illegal drugs are typically depicted in a unidimensional way that concentrates solely on their drug use. The resulting picture is all of use and frequency of drug use, effects of consumption, and problems stemming from "abuse". A natural consequent assumption is that all such "drug fiends" are atheistic predatory criminals, with no other interests than their drugs. The reality for young people in Britain today – as chronicled in a recent path-breaking book[21] – is that drug use has become "normalised", not least because drugs are consumed by normal people. To start, then, what part does Ecstasy play in the life of the users we questioned?

"…it's a part of it. I do other things…" (Euan)

"Yeah, but I would only say that it is a part of my social life…" (Naomi)

"I use it as part of my lifestyle…" (Iain)

"Yeah, well, I suppose it's part of the club scene … part of my lifestyle…" (Liz)

"it's a small part of it … it's only part of growing up…" (Phil)

Yet, for at least one of the small group (although perhaps not for ever), Ecstasy was somewhat more important:

"Yeah, it's a large part of it … and I think that if you took that away from me … I'd have a really shitty life…" (Fiona)

TAKING OTHER DRUGS

Drug use – of all kinds – is extensive in the large sample. Table 4.1 shows the percentages in each group who have used each listed substance in the year prior to interview. Cannabis use is, intriguingly, even more prevalent than tobacco.

Respondents in the large sample were also asked whether or not they used each of these drugs at the same time as they used Ecstasy, and the data is in Table 4.2. Irrespective of actual overall frequency of co-use, respondents also indicated whether they took each substance before, during or after taking Ecstasy. The only substance most often consumed *before* Ecstasy use was alcohol, although both cocaine and amphetamine were consumed nearly as often before Ecstasy use as during it. Those drugs used mostly *during* Ecstasy use were tobacco, solvents, mushrooms, LSD, poppers and ketamine. Those used predominantly *after* Ecstasy use were cannabis, heroin, temgesic, other opiates, temazepam, and other benzodiazepines.

Members of the small group were asked much the same questions: what other drugs they used simultaneously with the last Ecstasy tablet they used, and what other drugs they usually used with Ecstasy.

PERCENT USING OTHER DRUGS IN YEAR PRIOR TO INTERVIEW								
	ex-users	light stable	light erratic	medium stable	medium erratic	heavy stable	heavy erratic	**ALL**
n =	28	41	42	25	48	23	22	**229**
% alcohol	96	100	98	92	98	96	91	**97**
% cannabis	82	100	100	96	96	96	96	**96**
% tobacco	75	83	86	76	83	87	82	**82**
% amphetamine	35	80	83	76	94	91	91	**80**
% LSD	35	71	69	84	77	34	91	**71**
% cocaine	12	41	56	61	77	91	71	**58**
% poppers	19	47	38	65	65	48	52	**48**
% mushrooms	15	32	50	44	50	42	55	**42**
% temazepam	4	34	25	30	52	76	71	**40**
% benzodiazepine	8	17	15	22	33	56	35	**24**
% other opiate	–	9	7	39	21	13	40	**17**
% heroin	–	12	5	30	8	7	15	**10**
% ketamine	–	–	5	18	8	31	16	**9**
% temgesic	–	12	3	5	8	13	21	**8**
% solvent	–	5	8	4	10	6	10	**7**

Table 4.1

PERCENT USING OTHER DRUGS USED SIMULTANEOUSLY WITH MOST RECENT ECSTASY USE

	ex-users	light stable	light erratic	medium stable	medium erratic	heavy stable	heavy erratic	ALL
n =	28	41	42	25	48	23	22	229
% poppers	14	18	36	63	41	80	56	44
% temazepam	–	14	33	64	33	56	73	43
% amphetamine	12	22	40	44	34	57	55	38
% cocaine	40	11	15	35	33	47	50	31
% benzodiazepine	–	17	23	33	21	44	25	25
% ketamine	100	–	33	33	17	38	–	25
% LSD	12	6	16	41	22	17	35	20
% temgesic	100	–	–	–	10	25	40	19
% other opiate	–	13	17	13	23	–	25	16
% alcohol	9	5	10	21	9	22	14	12
% cannabis	–	5	18	4	9	27	16	11
% mushrooms	25	7	6	12	5	23	14	9
% tobacco	11	3	15	–	2	9	5	6
% heroin	–	–	–	–	–	–	20	3
% solvent	50	–	–	–	–	–	–	2

Table 4.2

In the small group, only one (Iain, a medium erratic user and a 20 year old employee) claimed that the last time he took Ecstasy he did so without taking any other drugs, and he added that although, "*more or less when I go out, I just take E by itself, but* [on] *a couple of occasions, I've taken speed with it.*" Further, only one (Fraser, the light erratic user who is a 43 year old employee) said that he would, "*normally … take E on its own*", yet he, too, added, "*although I have taken it with mushrooms, with acid, and with coke. And I've taken it while I've been smoking hash*". He continued, "*actually, good quality E on its own is probably best left un-interfered with, mushrooms seem to … eh, I had one experience with E and mushrooms, which was really … eh … a beautiful experience. Certainly, the one enhanced the other*".

All the others said that they used other drugs with Ecstasy both the last time they used Ecstasy, and "normally". Light users of Ecstasy seem to be comparatively heavier users of other drugs: for them, Ecstasy seems sometimes to be added to the other drugs taken apparently routinely. Frequently mentioned background drugs include alcohol, cannabis and amphetamines: occasional ones, LSD and cocaine. The only difference between stable and erratic light users seems to be that the stable users refer to their drug consumption as a fairly mundane matter, whereas the erratic Ecstasy users appear to follow rather more rigid – even ceremonial – consumption patterns. Apart from the consumption of alcohol and cannabis (and nicotine), light erratic users seem to prefer to separate rather than combine their use of the more exotic cocktails. Consider the remarks of Richie, a light erratic user (and a 30 year old employee):

"Taking E with maybe a couple of pints, and occasionally a joint or whatever ... which is mainly what I would call 'E by itself' ... or taking E with lots and lots of grass, lots of skunk, or whatever. That's about it. I haven't taken it with anything else ... though, normally, alcohol's generally in there, and cigarettes. Apart from that ... occasionally I really enjoy combining a lot of alcohol with Ecstasy if what I want to do is to be happy-drunk. But, if I'm taking Ecstasy, and going out to take Ecstasy ... have a couple of pints just to be social, you understand, but by and large, that's about it. If there's cannabis about, I'll smoke it. Last time I took E, actually, I was smoking a lot of very, very strong grass, and that was an interesting combination, but I was in the house, and I was up for that. There is still a big place for Ecstasy by itself. What I wouldn't mix it with is acid, which would be fucking stupid, or with speed, that would be pointless, or with anything else, with coke ... I like Ecstasy by itself..."

Medium users repeat the same pattern: stable users using Ecstasy on a background consumption of alcohol or amphetamines, and erratic Ecstasy users trying to separate one type of Ecstasy use from another, as in this example from Iain (a 20 year old employee):

"I took squares at the dancing, and then when I got to my pal's house, I took the doves but I didn't take the two Es at the dancing. I waited until the Aquarius [squares] had actually worn off me before I started taking the doves, but I took the two on the same night..."

Perhaps one way of conceptualising the difference between the stable and erratic users at this level of use is to see the stable users as adding Ecstasy to their more routine amphetamine use, and the erratic ones steering clear of amphetamine when using Ecstasy, and even being irritated when their Ecstasy appears to contain amphetamine. Heavier Ecstasy users confirm this pattern, and develop it in the sense that they use a greater number of substances, either consecutively (erratic users) or simultaneously (stable users) with Ecstasy, and are both more likely to mention specific substances taken to assist coming down from their Ecstasy use. A heavy stable user (Fiona, a 27 year old employee) commented:

"If you do poppers with E, when you sniff it [poppers] you feel so out of your box, when you come down off the poppers, you feel sober from the E. But the coke straightens up your head, and it makes your head a bit more giggly, lovely, and everything else ... and so the combination of the two, I think, makes you not quite sure what you are..."

Phil, a heavy erratic user (a 19 year old employee) put it like this:

"I started with speed, acid and alcohol, and downers after it [after taking the Ecstasy] ... Och! it was great! It was in a long stretch: it wasn't all at once, obviously. My sister gave us an acid, because I had no money ... before going to the disco, my sister gave me the acid, and I took it before I went out, so that when I went out, I was already tripping. When I was in, my pal came up and gave me some speed, and when that was finished, my other pal's like that: 'What are you on?', and I said that I'd done acid and speed, and he's like that: 'Well, here's an Eccy' ... and later I took that. It was a great night, and then I just went back to my flat, and then I had a half bottle of whisky. Obviously, I felt quite ... it's good when you're coming down off Ecstasy, you're like that, and you're taking drink, and it feels good when you're coming down off it ... I only took three jellies [temazepam] not straight with the whisky, it was after ... I don't usually touch jellies either. It's just because one my pals gave us them, and I was like that: 'Och well, I may as well just'..."

THE ECSTASY LIFESTYLE

How Ecstasy Fits in

Irrespective of how much Ecstasy they used (or for how long they had been using it), only one interviewee – Fiona, a 27 year old employee who is currently a heavy stable user – said anything that could even remotely be construed as indicative of some sort of cultural dependence on Ecstasy. She commented, when asked about the degree to which Ecstasy use was part of her lifestyle:

"Yeah, it's a large part of it ... and I think that if you took that away from me ... if you said 'You can never go out to a club again and never

take E again' … I'd have a really shitty life … because … I quite enjoy my work and everything, but I need more than that. I need a release, and that provides it for me … going out to a club or rave…"

Typically, all but the light users interviewed were careful to indicate that Ecstasy was a part of their lifestyle, but not necessarily a definitive or constitutive part of it. Here are some examples:

"…it's a part of it. I do other things…" (Euan, a 27 year old employee who is a light erratic user)

"Yeah, but I would only say that it is a part of my social life…" (Naomi, a 23 year old employee who is a light stable user)

"I use it as part of my lifestyle…" (Iain, a 20 year old employee who is a medium erratic user)

"Yeah, well, I suppose it's part of the club scene, which is part of my lifestyle…" (Liz, a 19 year old employee who is a medium erratic user)

"…it's a small part of it. It's not a major part of it because I wouldn't let it become a major part because it's nothing … it's only part of growing up. It's just me trying to enjoy my life. When I grow up, I've got more important things to worry about like my career and my job…" (Phil, a 19 year old employee who is a heavy erratic user)

Most of the other users denied that Ecstasy was even part of their current lifestyle. As Stuart said (a 28 year old student who is a light stable user), *"…not really, as I say, 'cos I haven't taken E for a couple of months … so, I mean, it's not really part of my lifestyle…"* Another (Richie, a 30 year old employee) was more indignant:

"I don't belong to the particular category which includes using Ecstasy. I use Ecstasy because it fits in with what I do. My lifestyle involves Ecstasy probably less than it involves sitting in the pub talking about politics. It involves Ecstasy less than it involves talking with fairly high ranking government officials. It's just one of the things I do. I don't belong to it, but I can fit in taking Ecstasy with the various things I do, you know, like going to the football, like whatever … meeting folk when I go to the pub or to work, all these sorts of things. I'm not an adherent to it. It doesn't dictate what I do. I doesn't particularly predict what I do. I don't think I can actually be predicted by my use of Ecstasy…"

The End of the Scene?

A few thought, however, that the "Ecstasy scene" would continue, even if they themselves were no longer part of it. This view was in the minority, but was not restricted to any particular type of user, as these three examples show:

"...it'll probably go on as long as it can. I can't see people stopping if they're in that kind of scene. There's no way they will stop, because it's part of the scene, kind of thing ... It will go on as long as it can..."
(Sharon, a 19 year old employee who is a light erratic user)

"I don't know if it will ever change. There will still be a lot of people doing E..." (Agnes, a 20 year old employee who is a medium stable user)

"Hopefully, it will be legalised, and you can have it tested and legally be able to test it in clubs, so that people know what's in them. It's not going to disappear. It will always be there..."
(Willie, a 24 year old unemployed man who is a heavy erratic user)

Others felt that the future of the Ecstasy scene lay out of the control of the participants. One, a 27 year old employee who is a light erratic user (Euan), thought it was a political issue:

"Em ... it depends on what the authorities make of it. I mean, they've shut down Hanger Thirteen [a night-club in Ayr, the location of three apparently Ecstasy related deaths in the mid 1990s] *so maybe they'll start planning on shutting down other venues, or make them play other sorts of music ... which would drive it* [the Ecstasy scene] *under-ground. But if they don't do that, then I think the music will flourish, and grow, and it will become the accepted night out across the country..."*

Moira (a 19 year old unemployed heavy stable user) pointed the finger elsewhere:

"I don't know ... If the media get their way, what will happen is that they'll get all the dancing shut down, and they'll just drive everything underground ... but that'll make it a lot easier for us to get on with it! Definitely! Because the scene was underground at the beginning, you know ... I'd like it to get back to what it was. For example, I was at a job

interview, and they're like that, 'What do you do in your spare time?' I was like that, 'Oh, I go to clubs'. 'What clubs do you go to?' And I'm like, 'Hanger Thirteen'. And they go, 'Oh'. Know what I mean? They're thinking, 'You must be one of those Ecstasy users'..."

A slightly larger group of interviewees simply thought the scene would deteriorate, along with the quality of available Ecstasy. Some saw the problem, but still felt that the dance scene was very durable, as did Kirsty, a 20 year old student who is a light stable user herself:

"I don't know. It's ... well ... you hear about a few years ago, how it [Ecstasy] used to be stronger, used to be better quality, and all the rest of it, and now it's cut with loads of rubbish, and as long as Es get seized when places get busted, it's just gonna get harder and harder to find it, and people are gonna make E with more and more rubbish in ... but I can't see the dance scene stopping for a good while yet..."

Or Morag, a 22 year old employee who is a medium stable user:

"I think it [scene] will keep going, but I think they will mix it [Ecstasy] with more and more crap, and I don't think it will be as strong as it used to be, so you're paying a lot of money, and will have less effect ... but I think it's going to get more and more widespread, because, I mean, who's not tried it?..."

Others were less optimistic: *"...it will just run its course eventually. I think it will deteriorate in form, and people will get sick of it..."* (Iain, a 20 year old employee who is a medium erratic user); or, *"...it will get worse, the Eccy will get worse. There will be more ... mixed in with them, and folk will want different drugs..."* (Phil, a 19 year old employee who is a heavy erratic user).

A final group thought that the current obsession with Ecstasy would be replaced, in time, by other, even as yet unknown, drugs: *"...I think it'll probably ... E will probably get replaced by something else. It was good E that was going about, then that might not be the case, but, I think ... yeah ... that will happen..."* (Gael, a 20 year old employee who is a light stable user). Others thought the scene would change, and thus survive:

"I think it's got to the state now where E and the dance scene are sort of inextricably linked, and one wouldn't exist without the other. I think E use will continue, but it might become unfashionable and be taken over by something else … coke's become a lot more fashionable, so that may take over from it. I think the dance scene will continue, but it will diverge into different forms … I mean, it has diverged into hundreds of different types of music, and different forms … I don't think it will die, as punk did, it's too big, in a way. It's become mainstream already…" (Liz, a 19 year old employee who is a medium erratic user)

Finally, here, one interviewee, Richie, even named the drugs that he felt would supersede Ecstasy:

"I've had this conversation, with one or two other folk about what's gonna become the next sort of big, the next big … shift in drug use in terms of what people are taking, and I'm not sure. The two obvious ones are both off-shoots of the E scene, one is to get more powerful hallucinogens like DMT, or something like that; or a return to mescaline or LSD making a comeback…"
(a 30 year old employee who is a light erratic user)

Using Ecstasy in the Future

As will be seen later (under the section on Quitting Ecstasy) many of these interviewees claim to have given up using Ecstasy by the time of their qualitative interview, although all but one had been active users at the time of the earlier quantitative interview.

When asked, in qualitative interview, whether or not they thought they would still be using Ecstasy in ten years' time, responses were mixed, with, perhaps surprisingly, the heaviest users being those most like to claim that they definitely not be using it. As Kath (a 25 year old employee who is currently a heavy stable Ecstasy user) put it:

"…if I don't [give up Ecstasy], I'll probably die. As I say, life's about moving up. I haven't got a plan. I'm not really sure where I'm going to end up, but I won't be taking E every weekend. It's like drinking. You get tired…"

The other heavy users said much the same. The medium level users were collectively or individually ambiguous. Most thought that, if anything, they would be using Ecstasy far less than at present, with Morag suggesting that she would only indulge on celebratory occasions:

"I will stop ... but, I don't know. If someone came up to me and said, 'Listen! It's your birthday' ... or whatever, 'You've not had this for 10 years!' ... maybe ... I don't know, maybe I'd be scared ... but, maybe, probably ... because you're always thinking about the first one ... 'Maybe it will be like that again' ... but it never is. I'd only try one out of curiosity, but it would only be the odd one, and that would be about it..." (22 year old employed medium stable user)

Other medium level users were more definite, even when prompted, as in this interchange:

"I don't think so. Emm ... In ten years time, I'll be 29. I'll probably ... em ... hopefully be a career type woman, where I'll be earning a lot of money, and being sensible, and doing grown up things. It just doesn't fit in. I mean, I could be married, with kids. I don't see myself going out at weekends ... em ... taking Ecstasy. I just don't see that happening ... ['Not even if you had a baby-sitter?'] *... No ... In a way, it's something that I enjoy doing because I'm young, and its part of being young. But I think there'll come a time, I don't know when, when I'll feel, in a way, too old for it. Or, I'll have grown out of it, or I'll be bored with it ... and if I'm not, it'll just happen naturally, but I don't see myself doing it when I'm 29..."* (Liz, a 19 year old employed medium erratic user)

Most of the light users, too, thought that they would have grown out of using Ecstasy within 10 years (although as one light erratic user, Danny, said, *"if you'd asked me 10 years ago if I'd still be smoking hash, I would have doubted it, but, you know, I still do"*), although nearly half of them thought, as one put it, that they would, *"still maybe like to try things occasionally"*, or as another claimed:

"I'd like to think, occasionally, yeah, whenever I fancied a wee treat for myself, maybe on your birthday you might take one. Or, when you're fed up with the wife, you'd take one..." (Euan, a 27 year old employed light erratic user)

So, what is the Ecstasy lifestyle? In a real sense, there isn't one. The members both of the large sample and the small group are just ordinary, normal people. They may do things that old adults don't do, but it is hard to otherwise distinguish them from the rest of their age peers. The difficulty with most research projects that investigate the use of illegal drugs is that far too many questions are asked about their drug use, and far too few about all the other things that they do. Thus, usually, when it comes to writing up the research results, it is hard to paint a rounded picture of people for whom, even in the most extreme cases – as in this sample – drugs only play a very small part in their lives.

What Else Do They Do?

However, recognising this in advance, we attempted to find out more about the other leisure pursuits and other interests of the large sample by asking them what other activities they get involved in (Table 4.3), what things do they regularly buy (Table 4.4), and how they would vote (Table 4.5) and whether or not they are religious (Table 4.6).

OTHER ACTIVITIES INDULGED IN AT LEAST MONTHLY (PERCENT OF WHOLE GROUP).								
visit/visited by friends friends	visit pubs	go to cinema or theatre	watch videos at home	have meal in restaurant	play sport	have a hobby	computer games	go to sports matches
100	93	88	86	81	69	62	38	28

Table 4.3

PURCHASES MADE AT LEAST MONTHLY (PERCENT OF WHOLE GROUP).						
sweets/ soft drinks	take away meals	records and/or CDs	magazines	broadsheet newspaper	tabloid newspaper	software disks
86	83	76	71	49	37	9

Table 4.4

VOTING INTENTIONS (PERCENT)						
Labour	None	SNP	Green	Conservative	LibDem	Other
42	23	15	8	5	4	4
Note: only 213 of the 229 answered this question						

Table 4.5

OFFENDING							
	ex-users	light stable	light erratic	medium stable	medium erratic	heavy stable	heavy erratic	ALL
n =	28	41	42	25	48	23	22	**229**
ever (*last year*)	%*(%)*	%*(%)*	%*(%)*	%*(%)*	%*(%)*	%*(%)*	%*(%)*	%*(%)*
ticket	89*(57)*	88*(59)*	86*(52)*	80*(68)*	81*(54)*	83*(48)*	86*(57)*	**85***(56)*
stolen	54*(25)*	56*(34)*	60*(31)*	56*(36)*	60*(40)*	61*(48)*	91*(71)*	**61***(39)*
shoplift	43*(10)*	53*(34)*	57*(21)*	48*(28)*	63*(29)*	48*(26)*	57*(29)*	**56***(26)*
fight	32*(10)*	51*(24)*	52*(29)*	58*(12)*	65*(35)*	52*(17)*	52*(29)*	**50***(24)*
deal	21*(19)*	54*(44)*	50*(38)*	44*(32)*	53*(47)*	48*(48)*	62*(48)*	**48***(40)*
vandal	21*(14)*	51*(29)*	29*(14)*	16*(–)*	35*(13)*	35*(17)*	57*(19)*	**35***(16)*
licence	29*(4)*	34*(17)*	21*(5)*	24*(4)*	27*(8)*	30*(4)*	43*(29)*	**29***(10)*
fiddle	14*(4)*	22*(12)*	29*(7)*	24*(–)*	15*(6)*	9*(4)*	24*(10)*	**20***(7)*
weapon	18*(4)*	32*(17)*	12*(7)*	12*(8)*	15*(13)*	13*(9)*	38*(24)*	**19***(11)*
bike	4*(–)*	7*(2)*	5*(2)*	4*(–)*	4*(–)*	9*(–)*	19*(10)*	**7***(2)*
mug	4*(–)*	5*(5)*	–*(–)*	–*(–)*	2*(–)*	–*(–)*	14*(5)*	**3***(1)*
sex	4*(4)*	4*(–)*	4*(–)*	–*(–)*	2*(–)*	–*(–)*	5*(–)*	**2***(–)*

Table 4.6

From Table 4.3, it is clear that these people are not just "drug fiends"! A healthy majority actively participate in sports (69%) or have hobbies (62%). Of course, like the rest of the nation, they watch videos, play computer games, go to the cinema or theatre, and even occasionally eat out (although they are more likely to spend their free time visiting, or being visited by, friends, or in pubs). They are (Table 4.4) not avid readers of tabloids, and are more likely to buy a broadsheet newspaper, although they are more likely to spend their money on records, CDs and magazines. Like the rest of the British population, they like sweets and soft drinks, and regularly buy take-away meals.

Their voting intentions (recall that these interviews were conducted between December 1993 and June 1995) are diverse, as shown in Table 4.5. Slightly more than half of them (52%) believe in the existence of some sort of superior beings, but only about a fifth of believers are active worshippers.

The Sins of Normal People

They are not, however, "saints". All were asked the following questions (first whether or not they had ever done them; then whether or not they had done each in the past 12 months), and their responses are in Table 4.6.

1. Travelled on a bus, tube or train without a ticket or having paid too low a fare ("ticket").
2. Bought or accepted things thought to be stolen ("stolen").
3. Taken things from shops or stores without paying ("shoplift").
4. Been involved in a physical fight with someone outside the family ("fight").
5. Sold drugs (other than Ecstasy) ("deal").
6. Deliberately damaged property such as a phone box, a car, a window, a street light (but without stealing anything) ("vandal").
7. Driven a car on a public road without a licence ("licence").
8. Fiddled an insurance claim ("fiddle").
9. Carried a weapon for self-protection or in case it was needed in a fight ("weapon").
10. Taken a bicycle with no intention of putting it back ("bike").
11. Taken money or something else from someone outside the family by using force or threats ("mug").
12. Been involved in the sex industry ("sex").

What can be made of this? First, with the possible exception of the heavy erratic users (who in most cases offend more frequently) there isn't much difference between the different user groups. Where differences do exist, they are not in a linear or even positive relation to the level or pattern of use. Second, note how high rates of lifetime and last year shoplifting, buying stolen goods and selling drugs other than Ecstasy are.

Some comparative data is available here from the Ecstasy-using respondents aged 16–44 questioned in the 1993 Scottish Crime Survey. The data has been recut for the purposes of Table 4.7 (although there is no comparable data on involvement in the sex industry or on dealing drugs other than Ecstasy). Levels of offending are slightly lower in the SCS sample (except for carrying an offensive weapon and being in a fight) but the overall picture is broadly the same.

Returning to buying stolen goods and selling drugs other than Ecstasy, some support for the veracity of this can be found in the answers that members of the large sample gave to questions about their sources of income and the directions in which it was spent. They were all asked directly how much money they made each week from, amongst other things, "crime" and "work on the side"; and later each

OFFENDING: OUR ECSTASY USERS AND THE SCS ECSTASY USERS		
n = ever *(last year)*	OUR Ecstasy Users 229 (%)	SCS Ecstasy Users 62 (%)
% ticket	85*(56)*	60*(22)*
% stolen	61*(39)*	49*(25)*
% shoplift	56*(26)*	35*(1)*
% fight	50*(24)*	53*(23)*
% vandal	35*(16)*	18*(3)*
% licence	29*(10)*	32*(7)*
% fiddle	20*(7)*	1*(4)*
% weapon	19*(11)*	27*(20)*
% bicycle	7*(2)*	–*(4)*
% mug	3*(1)*	1*(4)*

Table 4.7

was also asked how much each week they spent, again amongst other things, on "Ecstasy" and "other drugs". Their replies are in Table 4.8.

A good 30 per cent have some illegal income, and over 85 per cent make an illegal purchase on a weekly basis. Drugs account for much of the latter, but otherwise it is unclear what is bought, and from whom. However, while it is widely believed that "heavier" drug users (e.g., street injectors) regularly steal car radios, amongst other things, nobody has ever asked who buys them. Maybe this is at least part of the answer.

ILLEGAL TRANSACTIONS PER WEEK								
n =	ex-users 28	light stable 41	light erratic 42	medium stable 25	medium erratic 48	heavy stable 23	heavy erratic 22	**ALL** **229**
% no illegal income	68	81	73	84	63	74	50	**71**
% £1–£9 illegal income	21	17	17	4	13	11	18	**15**
% £50+ illegal income	11	2	10	12	25	16	32	**15**
% no illegal expenditure	54	15	7	8	6	9	9	**14**
% £1–£49 illegal expenditure	46	83	88	80	83	65	68	**76**
% £50+ illegal expenditure	–	2	5	12	10	26	23	**10**

Table 4.8

PROBLEMS WITH ECSTASY

As we mentioned earlier, extent of Ecstasy use was not related to lasting psychiatric problems in the large sample. A pattern of Ecstasy use involving heavier, more erratic use and bingeing might, however, be associated with increased report of adverse health consequences. Those in the large sample were asked about a range of problems possibly affected by Ecstasy and other drug use. They were asked whether they had ever felt unwell at a dance event, whether they had ever felt paranoid, whether they had ever experienced mood swings, felt depressed, had a seizure, lost their appetite or been unable to eat, been unable to sleep, had ever blacked out, or had had memory problems.

Related Illness

They were also asked how many days they had been ill (self-defined) in the previous year. This is shown in Table 4.9, where it can be seen that light users tended to report least illness (4–5 days per year), and heavy erratic users most illness (13 days per year), with other groups intermediate (6–7 days per year).

We looked at the different combinations of drugs used in the previous year to see if this could explain these various problems. We could divide the large sample into five groups: those who used alcohol and cannabis only; heavy cannabis users who also used stimulants and hallucinogens; heavy users of hallucinogens and stimulants; light users of opiates and benzodiazepines; and heavy users of opiates and benzodiazepines.

Three symptoms were related to these groups of drug users, but not specifically to Ecstasy use. These are shown in Table 4.10. It can be seen that the highest level users were more likely to report having expe-

AVERAGE DAYS OF ILLNESS PER YEAR BY ECSTASY USE PATTERN	
GROUP (n)	**Average**
Non-users & ex-users (28)	7.0
Light stable (41)	3.8
Light erratic (42)	4.8
Medium stable (25)	6.0
Medium erratic (48)	6.8
Heavy stable (23)	5.3
Heavy erratic (22)	12.7
ALL (229)	6.2

Table 4.9

rienced paranoia and memory problems. Higher level users were also
most likely to report having been general hospital in-patients in the
previous year, and were more likely to have been so because of drug-
related problems (of the 4 thus so admitted, 3 were at the highest use
level). None was a psychiatric in-patient.

One of the few things that stood out was that those eleven people
who reported having experienced appetite loss or eating difficulties
tended to report using more Ecstasy in the year than those who did not
report such symptoms.

Those who had experienced depression (self-defined) was related to
the drug use grouping shown in Table 4.10, and also to level of Ecstasy
use, days of alcohol use in the year, and total number of Ecstasy binges.
Those who reported depression drank on slightly fewer days (averaging
102 days) compared to those who reported no depression (averaging
128 days), but had binged on Ecstasy more often (the depressed averaged 3.8 binges; the non-depressed only averaged 1.9 binges). Fewer
users in the drug using groups 2 and 3 shown in Table 4.10 reported
depression than those who used only cannabis and alcohol, or who
used opiates and benzodiazepines. There was no clear relationship
between Ecstasy pattern and depression.

Ecstasy Problems in Perspective

Did the Ecstasy users in the small group think that Ecstasy had
changed them? Most thought not, and the few that agreed were more
likely to point to improvements than to deterioration. Only one, in
fact, thought that things had got worse, and even she (Agnes, a 20 year

NUMBER REPORTING SYMPTOMS BY LEVEL OF OVERALL DRUG USE			
Level of drug use	Was in-patient %	Was paranoid %	Had memory problems %
1 Cannabis/alcohol (n = 11)	9	36	9
2 Heavy cannabis/stimulants and hallucinogens (n = 40)	5	35	33
3 Heavy stimulants and hallucinogens (n = 73)	11	33	27
4 Opiates and benzodiazepines (n = 62)	7	47	53
5 Heavy opiates and benzodiazepines (n = 43)	21	54	44
Total group (n=229)	11	41	38

Table 4.10

old employed medium stable user) wasn't sure that it was a result of using Ecstasy. As she put it:

"I'm a lot more paranoid than I've ever been ... I used to be a lot ... I don't know if it's age ... but I used to be a lot clearer, like, of where I was going, and stuff ... no one would get in my way ... I was dead confident and ambitious ... but as time goes by, you collect more problems on the way ... it depends how life is going. As I say, we've had a talk about this, like with a couple of my pals who are, like, paranoid as well ... you know, about our boyfriends, but a wee bit more paranoid, quite touchy, you know, like saying something they might take it the wrong way, and you're like that, 'Calm down!' ... 'Stop being so para!' ... I don't know how many times we hear one another saying that. 'Oh, she's para!' ... 'He's para!' ... but we all smoke hash as well, so that might well have something to do with it..."

Thinking that Ecstasy had made a positive contribution was more likely, as in these three cases. Note how they, too, cannot always disentangle the effects of Ecstasy from the effects of age:

"I think about things in a different way ... I think it's made me more creative. I think it's made me more aware of ... it's just opened my mind, if you know what I mean ... I understand myself a lot better. Like, before I started taking E, I was just flakey. I didn't know I was flakey. Me was me ... that was the end of the story. But if I ... if I come up against a situation in life, and I'm feeling a certain way, I know why it is. I can understand the way it is, and I can train myself to think positive, you know. Like freaking out over a job interview, you know. Like, I'll go, 'Right! This is cool: it happens to everybody' ... and it helps me look at life like that..." (Gael, a 20 year old employee who is a light stable user)

"It's opened me up a lot more. I used to be shy. That could be age, I suppose. I don't know if it's the E that's done it ... I certainly was shy. But meeting folk while I was on it, you were more open ... and it just stayed with me, you know, being more open with folk..." (Danny, a 21 year old employed light erratic user)

"I value myself a lot more, because I didn't have much of an opinion of myself, when I was getting drunk and going away with all these guys and stuff. I've got a lot more respect for myself now, and I care a lot more about the world I live in, and my friends mean a lot more to

me than they did then. But I don't know if that's me just getting older. I don't really know if it's related to E…" (Fiona, a 27 year old employed heavy stable user)

Neither did most appear to know anybody who had been adversely affected by taking Ecstasy. Indeed, the most common response to this question was either a curt *"no"* or a sarcastic riposte. Willie, for example (a 24 year old unemployed man who is a heavy erratic user) replied:

"I know lots of people with problem drug use, yeah. Alcohol, tobacco … I don't know anyone with a problem with E at all. I don't think E warrants having a problem on it, you know…"

A few more claimed to have heard about someone who had a problem with Ecstasy (*"I know of a guy who did have a problem"* or *"I heard of a guy, but not personally"*), but this rarely rose above hearsay. Only one knew of someone apparently damaged by Ecstasy, but recalled also that the damage was temporary:

"…there's one guy in particular that I've only met a couple of times, and when you try to have a conversation with him, it's a total night-mare. You'd be like that: 'Are you going out tonight?' and he'd be like that, 'No' … you know? Just hiding, yeah … I reckon he knows he's paranoid … and a bit vacant … like attention span-wise, you know what I mean? You're chatting to them one minute, and they might be a bit sort of … you know, gold fish memory … most people I know that have taken too much of it … their head got a bit scrambled, and they stopped taking it…" (Gael, a 20 year old employee who is a light stable user)

Most of those interviewed were, in fact, hard pressed to think of any negative effect that Ecstasy had had. A few suggested weight loss, but, again, they were unsure whether or not this was because of the dancing, or the accompanying Ecstasy.

QUITTING ECSTASY

"Quitting" is a difficult concept to establish. Some of the lighter Ecstasy users often go months at a time without using any Ecstasy, and might never take another tablet. Conversely, some of the erstwhile heaviest users might currently be abstinent, but could well take up

Ecstasy use again in the future. This is shown in Table 4.11, which reports the answers from the Ecstasy-using members of the large group when they were asked if they had ever given up using Ecstasy.

A perhaps surprisingly large number (41 per cent) of the large sample claim to have given up using Ecstasy at some time or other (although none would claim that this is currently a permanent step) and a slightly larger number – 52 per cent – say that they intend to give up in the future. Why had so many given up in the past? The most frequently cited reason (by 32, 39% of the temporary abstainers) was "bad side effects", followed by 13 (16%) citing "bad comedown", which might be felt to be much the same thing. Ten more (12%) said that their circumstances had changed, another 10 that they had lost interest, and a further 10 that the low quality of the available Ecstasy had put them off. Seven (9%) gave a variety of other reasons. Those who thought that they might give up using Ecstasy at some time in the future gave slightly different reasons. The most commonly expected reason was "boredom" (cited by 26%), followed by another 17% who thought they would mature out of using Ecstasy. Eleven per cent thought they would grow out of the dance scene, another 11% that their circumstances would change, and a further 11% that the poor quality of available Ecstasy would put them off. Ten per cent thought that health worries would make them quit, and the rest (14%) couldn't think of a reason.

Temporary Abstinence

As we already mentioned, quitting might be temporary or permanent. Table 4.12 shows that temporary abstemiousness is not just the province of light users, or just of erratic ones. A variety of

GIVING UP ECSTASY								
	ex-users	light stable	light erratic	medium stable	medium erratic	heavy stable	heavy erratic	**ALL**
n =	8	41	42	25	48	23	22	209
% ever given up	100	44	43	32	46	13	32	**41**
% given up once only	100	37	36	16	19	4	5	**25**
% given up more than once	–	7	7	16	17	9	27	**15**
% intend to give up in future	–	27	50	68	52	78	73	**52**

Note: 20 non-users excluded from this table.

Table 4.11

reasons were given for temporarily given up. These ranged from financial reasons (18%), changed circumstances (17%), lack of interest (15%), concern about health effects (12%), "needing a break from Ecstasy" (8%), the poor quality of Ecstasy (8%), no real reason (7%), grown out of the dance scene (6%), and various other reasons (9%).

In the small group, the one ex-user (unemployed 22 year old Charlie) is not the only one to have "quit" Ecstasy, although the fact that he has now been an ex-user for such a long time allows more confidence in the permanence of his abstinence. His story:

"I've not used it since. I didn't want to. Very shortly after that [binge], I lost it completely. I mean, I didn't want to stop taking E. Things were fine. I had my ups, and I had my downs, but in March 1993, I went away, and decided not to take any ... That was about 3 months. I made the conscious effort not to take any, and then I just lost it. I just lost the place completely. Was scared to go to sleep at night. Thought I wasn't breathing. Feeling very anxious. Felt as if I took a nervous breakdown ... I don't think it was just E. I had a lot of stress in my life, and then I realised that I couldn't take E. My physical body just couldn't handle it, and I became very sensitive to things ... I cannae blame the E. It was my life. It was really stressful. I never had a job. I was going out with a girl that caused me a lot of grief. Erm ... a lot of father stuff. I hadn't spoken to my father for a long time. Eh ... a lot of betrayal through male friends ... the first time was physical. This was more of a mental thing. Anxiety, and stuff like that..."

ABSTAINING FROM ECSTASY							
	ex-users	light stable	light erratic	medium stable	medium erratic	heavy stable	heavy erratic	**ALL**
n =	8	39	39	25	44	23	21	**199**
% abstained 1–2 months	–	8	18	64	48	83	52	**39**
% abstained 3–6 months	–	41	54	28	39	13	38	**36**
% abstained 6–48 months	100	51	28	8	14	4	10	**25**

Note: 20 non-users excluded from this table.

Table 4.12

The others were all asked if they had "ever consciously given up Ecstasy". Bear in mind here that although all 21 were "users" when participating in the quantitative phase of the project, and were interviewed between December 1993 and June 1995, a few had not used for several months prior to that first interview. Further, the qualitative interviews were conducted in August and September 1996, well after the lengthy quantitative phase had concluded. So, all were interviewed qualitatively at least a year after, and up to two and a half years after their initial quantitative interview.

Of the four light stable users, only one claimed never to have had a period of abstinence. The other three had all stopped at least once, but for different reasons. Stuart (a 28 year old student) told himself:

"Aye, I've said, 'I'm not going to take them any more' ... like, after that guy had a fit, you know ... it was the fright of seeing what it's done to someone else ... that lasted a couple of months ... then we all just really, we all just went out and took it again. I give it up every time I stop, really..."

Gael (a 20 year old employee) had temporarily quit (she was using Ecstasy at the time of interview) because she:

"...was getting worried that I was getting a sort of serious sort of psychological addiction to it ... because I felt that I couldn't go to a club unless I was Eeed, and that ... um ... my night was spoiled if I wasn't Eeed, and I had a few personal problems at the time, also ... and I thought, 'Right, I think now would be a good time to stop for a few months' ... and I stopped for 4 months, and it was easy. I think that I just wanted to be able to comfort myself with the thought that if I wanted to stop, I could..."

The third (Naomi, a 23 year old employee):

"...took one half of an E once, and I had a bad experience on it, and I didn't take it for a long time after that. I thought I was going to pass out in a club, and I had to leave really quickly, and I was sick, and ... erm ... I thought, 'Why am I doing this?' ... I felt as if I was about to faint ... I think it was a mixture of both not drinking water, and the E, and the club was hot and packed. I stopped for about a year or so, and then, I was out with friends, and they'd got one, and I took a tiny little bit off one, and then I was fine on it, and it was alright. And I had a

few beers ... and a wee bit of it made me dance a wee bit, so it was nice. So, then, you know, gradually, after a wee while, I took a half, a wee while after that ... but ... em ... that's how I started again, by just taking a tiny wee bit from somebody..."

Permanent Cessation

Three of the light erratic users claimed to have given up permanently. Sharon (a 19 year old employee) had experienced kidney problems which she put down to her use of Ecstasy and amphetamines. She claimed to have used neither for a year prior to interview. The second, Danny, (a 21 year old employee) recalled that:

"Basically, yes ... for 6 months now ... just basically not interested in it at all ... I've been offered it, but turned it down ... no interest for it. When I look back three years ago, 1993 ... eh! I could never go back to that! It was a phase. It was good at the time. I look back on it, I'm not ashamed of what I did. I'm glad I tried it, but like everything, some things are in, and then some things go out again. Something else's round the corner: what it is, I don't know ... Well, if it was another drug, I wouldn't be taking it ... Yeah. E and speed times are over, finished..."

The other light erratic user who had given up (Fraser, the 43 year old employee) said that he'd been off Ecstasy for a year:

"In the initial year, 1989, from about February, right through, I took E on about 30 occasions; the next year, I took on about 20 occasions. That was 1990, it was a bit of a duff year, and I thought the scene would take off then, but it didn't. The scene took off in 1991, that year it went totally bananas. That year I probably did about 50 Eees. I was probably doing E once a week, and by that time it was pretty endemic. 1992? Yeah, still quite high, but for me the rot had set in. The scene had already got heavy, there was violence ... the bad vibes, and all the rest of it. But I still remember about 30 occasions in 1992; and then in 1993 down to about 20 occasions, and then it was the last ... the last kind of blast of it, really, to me. That's when it totally finished. Although in 1994, I was out maybe about 4 or 5 times. I still took E, with less pleasure attached to any of it because, you know, things come and go. The scene has been and gone ... and ... the last time I took it ... that was 1995, but I was aware of those kind of depressions that had probably been happening for a year or two ... and I thought,

'there is nothing in my life to make me feel that bad' ... so, I thought the drug must have been responsible for it..."

Sporadic Moderation

Two more light erratic users were unable to distinguish their normal using pattern from the suggested one of interspersing indulgence and abstention. One, Richie (a 30 year old employee) felt that he should be *"very sparing about any sort of drug, including alcohol"*, and reduced his intake of everything occasionally; and the other (Euan, a 27 year old employee) would regularly refuse an offered Ecstasy tablet because, as he put it:

"I don't want to be dependent on this certain person giving me it, or being in the position of having taken it two or three times in a row, which I'd rather not do. It's probably a lot to do with people thinking you're a drug addict; or people thinking your life is controlled by drugs. You don't want people thinking that. If attitudes were different, then you might take it every weekend. But because of the way that people's attitudes are, then you can't take it all the time because people will, like when you're in a responsible position, then they will say you're a 'mad druggy that can't be trusted' ... so you need to avoid that..."

Of the two medium stable users who responded to this question, both had given up Ecstasy. Agnes, a 20 year old employee, claimed that *"...you grow out of Ecstasy..."*, because, for her, she:

"...couldn't handle the Sundays any more. The depression. It can make you really depressed ... and then trying to get back to work. You don't straighten up, I'd say, until Tuesday ... it's not hard to just stop and do something else. Get a carry out, sit in the house with one of your pals. It's not hard..."

The other, Morag, a 22 year old employee, could no longer handle the come-downs. She recalled:

"I've not taken it for a long time ... I've not taken it since the New Year, that was the last one. Until then I was taking it a lot. But I've totally stopped now. I've not been to a club for a while ... I feel as if it's taken it's toll ... I mean, a lot of folk say it'll not do you any harm, and all the rest of it, but I feel as though it is taking it's toll, and to be

honest, I'm fed up with that ... I've done it [Ecstasy] *for a while now.
Did it for about five years. I'm sick to death of the scene, and just want
something different now ... And I do feel better now that I have
stopped for a while. Because I was ... like, getting ... em ... on a
Sunday when you were coming down ... depressions which lasted for a
couple of days, and then it was really like the Tuesday or the
Wednesday before you were starting to feel back to yourself, and it
was taking longer and longer for me to feel normal again. Some folk it
doesn't effect like that, and some folk it does. But I used to get really
depressed. I wouldn't go out of the house. I wouldn't go down to the
shop. I wouldn't go out in public at all ... just sat in the house and
smoked hash ... I feel as if I'm getting to an age where I should be
doing more sensible things. Like, if I go to a club, it's a lot younger
people, and they're having a great time like you used to have when you
first started going out, and you think, 'This is not the same any more',
and my health, that makes me feel guilty about it. But I definitely think
I've outgrown it. It's just not the same buzz any more. It's just not as
interesting..."*

Neither of the two medium erratic users had ever felt that they had
consciously given up Ecstasy, although, of course, their pattern of use is
one of alternating use with abstention. Liz, a 19 year old employee,
said that she only abstained *"if I'm quite broke"*, and the other, Iain, a
20 year old employed male, related his periods of abstention to relationships as well as to resources:

"[I've] ... *not given it up as such. After the first time I tried it, I never
touched it for 18 months. It wasn't due to the fact that I didn't want
to, it was due to the fact that I just didn't have the money for it, and it
was due to the fact that I wasn't going to the dancing. I met a girl, and
I started going out with her, and I was basically so in love with her that
I didn't see any of my pals for about 14 months. I hardly saw them.
She wasn't into the same kind of music that I was into, so we ... spent
a lot of time in the pub. But once I finished with her, I started seeing
my pals again, and I started going to the dancing again, and I started
taking it again..."*

Endless Indulgence

The three heavy stable users all denied every consciously giving up
Ecstasy. One of them, Kath, a 25 year old employee, explained:

"No, I don't think I'd need to do that ... because I don't think it's a problem. I don't think it's something you have to give up, because it will just filter out, you know what I mean? I don't think I'll club for the rest of my life, but when I stop clubbing, I don't think I'll stop taking E entirely. But I don't think I'll take it more than once a year, whatever ... If I'm at a party, and some friend of mine says, 'Listen! I've got some Eees. Do you want to remember what it was like when you were younger?' I would ... You always think ... like when I left University, I thought I'd magically turn into a sensible person, and have my mortgage, give up smoking, never drink. That hasn't happened yet, but it will, because I get tired ... I get bored, of clubbing. I get very bored of club nights now. Going out constantly, it's not the be all and end all..."

Unlike the other erratic users, the two heavy erratic users both denied ever consciously giving up Ecstasy, although one of them (Willie, a 24 year old unemployed man) recognised that others – not himself – were *"getting burnt out on E"*.

Overall, there is a curious contradiction between the fact that although so few found Ecstasy use to be problematic – particularly when first interviewed – so many (at least of the small group) had quit by the time we had got round to re-interviewing them. Of course, several years had elapsed between the two interviews, and we have no reason to suppose the later experiences of the small group might be representative of the feelings and actions of the large sample. Nevertheless, there is more than a hint that for many we spoke to, growing out of Ecstasy use was a metaphor for growing out of the club and rave scene, indeed for growing up itself.

Remember Gael from Chapter Three, speaking when she was aged 20, of the scene which had bypassed her now, as it was *"full of 12 year old ravers"*? The strong link between Ecstasy-related activity (chiefly strenuous all-night dancing) might well foster abstinence among those who find the drug itself unproblematic. Another possibility, suggested to us by Michael Morgan,[22] is that with age the amount of serotonin in the brain naturally tends to decrease. So, as users age they may come to feel less affected by Ecstasy. They tend to attribute this to the drug being weaker, or to a less satisfactory scene, rather than to changes in themselves of which they are unaware.

In the final chapter, we report what we found when we interviewed 7 members of the small group again in 1999. For some of them, this was nearly 6 years after we had first interviewed them. Were they still attending Ecstasy-fuelled raves? Or had they settled down?

NOTES
[21] Parker, H., Aldridge, J. & Measham, F., **Illegal Leisure: The normalisation of adolescent recreational drug use**, Routledge, London, 1998.
[22] Personal communication.

CHAPTER FIVE
Ecstasy – Impressions
and Reality

Evening Times, 28.02.90.

Over the period that we were researching, the popular media waged a sustained campaign of vilification against Ecstasy. Before we move to finding out where our small group has got to, a reminder of some of their views. The one issue that they were almost universally condemnatory about was coverage of Ecstasy use in the media. Part of the reason was the perceived overreaction of coverage:

"Erm ... I think the tabloid press has had a complete overreaction and moral panic about it..." (Liz)

"...it's overblown, and most of it is negative, it's very negative ... 'Killer drug' ... bla! bla! ... bla! ... it dehydrates you and kills people..." (Willie)

"A bit hysterically, yeah. Em ... I think it's just sort of ... yeah ... they exploit cases of like, maybe, of like terror or whatever, and they put it in a bad light. They make it into some sort of panic thing to sell papers..." (Naomi)

Another part was the apparent hypocrisy:

"I think the way the papers ... like the Sun ... like it's disgusting. I was reading a thing, and it was saying that, like, Britain was a Brewery

State ... you know. And the problem for them is that the young people are not going out and getting pissed every night. It means that the breweries are losing loads of money ... Yeah, the young people are going out and taking E, and the breweries are losing wads of cash. I think the papers are on their side, so they make it like 'Death and Evil', and 'Bad' ... so they scare monger people into going back to getting pissed and keeping the breweries happy..." (Fiona)

"Well, it's a good story, you know. It's sex and drugs and rock and roll. Eh? It sells papers, but it's sensationalised and it's trivialised ... Ecstasy is just the new demon, and it's the same old hypocritical crap..." (Fraser)

WHAT DID THEY KNOW?

All respondents in the large sample were asked to rate various sources of information about Ecstasy using a five point scale from "rubbish", through "poor" to "50/50" to "good" and finally to "excellent". Their responses are in Table 5.1.

The "media" were not highly regarded by members of the small group (as we saw at the beginning of this chapter). Nor were the media much liked by members of the large sample, although magazines, drug leaflets and friends scored well – something which the separate research we conducted on the information needs of Ecstasy users bears out (see the Appendix).

This is not unexpected, as any even brief look at media coverage would suggest. Indeed, although we didn't systematically scour newsprint for mentions of "Ecstasy", we have been filing away odd items since the late 1980s. A first conclusion from looking at this batch of clippings is that newspaper coverage of Ecstasy has been surprisingly imaginative. Here is

PERCENT RATING SOURCES OF INFORMATION ON ECSTASY					
	Television	Tabloids	Broad-sheets	Magazines	Drug leaflets	Friends
n =	220	220	180	204	169	222
rubbish	20	67	14	3	1	3
poor	46	26	36	11	5	6
50/50	25	5	34	37	17	32
good	9	2	15	46	59	47
excellent	–	–	1	3	18	12

Table 5.1

a variety of headlines culled from just a few newspapers. All these sub-editors have, of course, read Irving Stone's 1961 novel:

"THE AGONY OF ECSTASY" *Daily Mirror*, 02.09.92.
"THE AGONY OF ECSTASY" *Daily Record*, 22.09.92.
"THE AGONY AFTER ECSTASY" *Manchester Evening News*, 27.01.93.
"PARENTAL AGONY AND THE ECSTASY" *Independent on Sunday*, 11.04.93.
"ECSTASY OR AGONY?" *Guardian*, 07.09.93.
"ECSTASY THAT LEADS TO AGONY" *Scotland on Sunday*, 18.09.94.
"ECSTASY AND THE AGONY" *Guardian*, 19.03.95.
"THE AGONY OF ECSTASY" *Independent*, 14.11.95.
"AGONY IN ECSTASY" *Sun*, 15.11.95.
"THE AGONY OF THE ECSTASY" *Sunday Mail*, 19.11.95.
"PATHOLOGISTS UNCOVER AGONY OF ECSTASY" *Herald*, 13.02.96.
"THE AGONY OF ECSTASY" *Evening Times*, 14.06.96.
"THE AGONIES OF ECSTASY" *Herald*, 14.11.96.
"AGONY BOUND TO FOLLOW THE ECSTASY" *Herald*, 16.12.96.
"THE AGONY OF ECSTASY" *Daily Mail*, 18.02.97.
"THE AGONY OF ECSTASY" *Guardian*, 05.07.97.
"THE ECSTASY AND THE AGONY" *Independent*, 12.10.97.
"PARENTS' AGONY AFTER ECSTASY" *Evening Times*, 22.12.97.

A second conclusion is a vast overemphasis on death. Not just in the excessive reporting of apparent Ecstasy-related fatalities, but the frequent and generally careless use of words like "deadly" and "killer" and the repeated use of such hackneyed phrases as "dancing with death" and "dicing with death". Some more examples:

"COCKTAIL OF DEATH: WARNING ON KILLER DRUG" *Evening Times*, 08.12.87.
"DEADLY DRUGS RIP-OFF AT THE DISCO" *Daily Record*, 01.03.89.
"FROM ECSTASY TO DEATH AND DESPAIR" *Guardian*, 29.11.91.
"RAVERS PLAY 'RUSSIAN ROULETTE' WITH ECSTASY" *Independent*, 28.12.91.
"A NIGHT OF ECSTASY, A TASTE OF DEATH" *Evening Standard*, 14.01.92.
"THE EVIL MEN WHO TRADE IN TABLETS OF DEATH" *Sunday Mail*, 08.03.92.

"DANCING WITH DEATH" *Daily Record*, 04.06.92.
"ECSTASY KIDS ARE DICING WITH DEATH" *Daily Record*,
23.09.92.
"DANCING WITH DEATH" *Daily Record*, 30.11.93.
"THE DANCE WITH DEATH" *Evening Times*, 15.02.95.
"RAVE RAID AS DANCE OF DEATH GOES ON" *Daily Record*,
21.02.95.
"TRAIL OF DEATH" *Sunday Mail*, 19.11.95.
"ECSTASY DISCO GIRL DANCES WITH DEATH" *Daily Express*,
04.01.96.
"DANCE OF DEATH" *Scotland on Sunday*, 14.04.96.

Most recently, the broadsheets seem to have taken more of a lead, particularly by repackaging apparently definitive scientific studies which originally appeared in popular science magazines. The fact that brain scans can pick up what seem to be temporary changes in pictorial representations of the brains of a handful of Ecstasy users is never allowed to get in the way of a good story. So:

"ACID EATS THE BRAIN LOOSE" *Guardian*, 01.11.88.
"ECSTASY WILL BEND YOUR BRAIN" *Daily Record*, 26.09.94.
"ECSTASY BRAIN DAMAGE FEARS" *Sunday Post*, 05.03.95.
"RAVE DRUG MAY DAMAGE THE BRAIN" *New Scientist*, 02.09.95.
"ECSTASY USERS 'RISKING LONG-TERM BRAIN DAMAGE'"
Independent, 14.06.96.
"ECSTASY 'CAUSES BRAIN DAMAGE'" *Evening Times*, 14.06.96.
"ECSTASY WILL ROT YOUR BRAIN" *Daily Record*, 14.06.96.
"PROOF POSITIVE. TAKING ECSTASY PERMANENTLY ALTERS
YOUR BRAIN" *Independent*, 06.11.97.
"THE MENTAL AGONY OF ECSTASY" *Times Higher*, 20.03.98.
"MEMORY IS DAMAGED BY ECSTASY" *Independent*, 21.12.98.

For example, just take one of these ("PROOF POSITIVE. TAKING ECSTASY PERMANENTLY ALTERS YOUR BRAIN" *Independent*, 06.11.97). This originated with an article in the *New Scientist* (08.11.97) which was headed, "DOES ECSTASY CAUSE LASTING DAMAGE TO THE HUMAN BRAIN?" The *New Scientist* article quoted a member of the original research team as saying, of Ecstasy, "the message is that if you're going to use it, do it in moderation". In the abstract reporting the original research, the words "long-lasting", but not the word "permanent" appears. The study presented data from

14 Ecstasy users and 8 controls. The users were believed to be "very heavy" users, but no confirmation tests were undertaken. And so on.

Over this latter period (although it started earlier), the tabloids seem to be taking a different tack. Now no longer attacking the normal people who use normal Ecstasy, they concentrate on unusual people (chiefly the young) and abnormal Ecstasy (new "super strength" Ecstasy, or adulterated or fake tablets), as in these:

"FAKES ARE THE BIGGEST ECSTASY DANGER" *Herald*, 10.01.92.
"PERIL OF THE FAKE ECSTASY" *Daily Record*, 04.06.92.
"TOT, AGE TWO, ON ECSTASY" *Sun*, 13.02.93.
"ECSTASY NIGHTMARE OF DRUGGED TODDLER" *Daily Star*, 23.04.93.
"BOGUS DRUGS MIX TO HOOK THE RAVE KIDS" *Daily Record*, 23.04.93.
"DOC TREATS ECSTASY VICTIMS AGED 11" *Daily Record*, 13.09.94.
"'PARTY PACKS' PUT YOUNGSTERS AT RISK ON THE TECHNO-DANCE SCENE" *Scotsman*, 13.09.94.
"KIDS OF 13 AT DEATH RAVE" *Daily Record*, 14.02.95.
"TRIPLE STRENGTH ECSTASY SEIZED" *Herald*, 28.10.95.
"KILLER ECSTASY ALERT" *Daily Record*, 30.10.95.
"PARTY DRUG KITS FOR £50. POLICE FEARS ON SUPER E" *Daily Record*, 06.11.95.
"DEADLY SUPER E DRUG SEIZED IN CLUB" *Daily Record*, 27.11.95.
"SUPER DRUG ALERT – POLICE WARN NEW ECSTASY IS LETHAL" *Daily Record*, 25.10.96.
"NOW DEADLY DEALERS LACE RAVE PILLS WITH HEROIN" *Evening Times*, 08.11.96.
"CUT-PRICE ECSTASY FLOODING MARKET" *Independent*, 19.04.97.
"POLICE FEARS OVER DEADLY NEW ECSTASY" *Daily Record*, 21.10.97.

It is never clear how much influence reporting like this has on users, but we did ask all members of the large sample how they learned about the various physical, psychological and legal hazards of taking Ecstasy. They were allowed to give as many hazards of each type as each chose, so it is difficult to present the data in the usual tabular manner. However, as for physical hazards, "overheating" and/or "dehydration" received 109 mentions; "fatigue", 76 mentions, and the media-popular hazards of "brain damage" and/or "sapping spinal fluid" only 21 mentions. As for psychological hazards, "depression" got 64 mentions; "paranoia" 57; "mood swings" 25; "concentration" and/or "memory" problems 16; and "anxiety", 6. As for legal hazards, the fact that it is a "class A" substance received 122 mentions, but the large number of types of disposal believed to be risks of Ecstasy use if caught indicate widespread confusion.

All members of the large sample were also asked where they got such information on hazards, and, finally, which type of hazard was the most dangerous. Their replies are in Table 5.2.

A few observations can be made. First, although drug users commonly prefer knowledge from friends, and typically despise the "media", a surprisingly large number claim to get their information from the latter rather than from the former. Second, this is mostly the case for legal hazards, but is still true for a third for physical hazards, and for nearly a quarter for psychological hazards. Third, the legal hazard is arguably the most significant (Ecstasy being a Class A substance) but is only seen so by a third: more think the psychological hazards to be the worst.

WHERE ARE THEY NOW?

In early 1999, we decided to try – with no funds and only a limited amount of time – to track down as many of the small group as we could, and see what they were up to. It wasn't a great success: we had telephone numbers, but quite a few of the group had moved on in the past 4 years (all had initially been interviewed as members of the large sample between April 1994 and early January 1995), and none seemed to have left forwarding addresses. But we were able to re-contact seven members of the small group, and all of them agreed to allow us to interview them again. They were Fraser, Stuart, Richie, Danny, Agnes, Sharon and Moira.

SOURCES OF INFORMATION ON THE HAZARDS OF ECSTASY					
%	Friends	Own experience	Media	Other	Worst hazard
Physical	25	32	36	7	25
Psychological	20	48	23	9	43
Legal	27	20	45	8	32

Table 5.2

We asked them whether or not they were still using Ecstasy, and if not, why not.

First, Fraser. When we first interviewed him, he was our oldest interviewee. He was then a daily cannabis user, and occasionally used cocaine, amphetamines, mushrooms and LSD. When we later talked to him in early 1999, he told us that he had given up Ecstasy altogether:

"I'm 47 now, and I don't take E any more ... just a personal choice. Change of lifestyle basically, but lots of other reason as well ... in terms of the quality went down. I mean the scene, as such, that I was involved in has passed and finished ... and I finished with it ... eh ... on a regular basis about 2 or 3 years ago. The last, I'd had, would have been in '98. It would be some time last summer. Not even going to a rave. It was just actually going to a talk in Edinburgh. I did that, and it was pretty mental ... It was kind of on the bus, you know, I had it on the bus..."

Fraser continued:

"Later he [the speaker] *was talking about the acid days, and 'We hear about rave culture' and I'm going 'Aye it's dead, finished'. The personal reasons for giving up were that I'd played it through really, you know. For me it was finished ... but just in terms of my lifestyle choices. I'm ... it's a long time that I've been taking drugs you know, and it's just, well that's it. I've had enough ... it's fairly recent. The total stop! That includes hash, and includes anything psychoactive. Alcohol too, but not tobacco. Yes, the end of last summer was my last thing..."*

Later still, he told us:

"I made a decision just recently to stop taking all the psychoactive substances. That was just personal choice. I was just taking a different direction in my life. I found I was spiritually stagnating. In terms of my own personal growth. So that was the reason. There was just ... instead of, initially when I was taking most of these drugs I was looking for a certain amount of seeking, and certain amount of pleasure but there was also another dimension to it in terms of consciousness expansion and all the rest of it. And that stopped. It just doesn't work for me any more ... it just became a habit, and when it becomes

a habit it's time to stop. So I made that decision. The 'games a bogie'
[end of the road]: *get clean for the millennium thanks very much! ... So*
it's a combination of social factors and at the end of the day a certain
amount of ... it can point in the right direction but it's not going to
give you the answer..."

Stuart is 32 now. Never a heavy user of Ecstasy, does he still use it at
all?

"I haven't taken E for a few months. Since I've done the survey, I think
I've done a couple of Eees and I think that was a few years ago. Yes,
'cos it's well ... it's not the same as it was before, you know, the quality
... or how it affects your mind. Giving up was, um, it's been more of a
decision really ... just through myself ... just observing, reading articles
in papers, and making logical decisions from information you get in
the media ... and what you see is happening round about you. There's
been a couple of, there's two reasons that has put me off them. One is
the chemical effect and the psychological effect it has on you some-
times. E can be great, okay? But there are situations within that experi-
ence when you do feel very vulnerable. Right? And then you come
down from the feeling, but the fact that you knew you were vulnerable,
you were actually like, getting abused, from the situation. Like so
people who have maybe caused that effect on you might not even
know, you might just have been tuning in on a gesture, or look or
whatever, that's caused that. So that's one reason for it because I've
had a couple of experiences like that and it sort of spoils the whole
effect..."

We asked him what these experiences were:

"It's just a couple of experiences I've had. Like I was at a gig once, and
I was in the toilets and there were some neds in the place who were
obviously heavy drinkers, you know, jellied up [having taken
temezepam], *jellied and bevvied or something like that. So they were*
violent and I was Eeeing. It left me in quite a volatile situation and I
was sort of oblivious to it, you know. Yeah, I just walked out but I was
lucky 'cos I could easily have had my head smashed in. It's situations
like that ... and it causes difficulties in relationships as well: jumping
into bed and sleeping around and that creates complications as well. So
you've got to weigh up ... em I think, aye, I don't think it's a good idea
to take E within a relationship because to get good experiences in a

relationship you really need to work at it. If you take drugs all the time, you're high, and you're not going to feel ... together..."

Richie, now 34, had never been a heavy Ecstasy user either, and he, too, had now stopped. But unlike Fraser, he was carrying on with other drugs, particularly alcohol. Why had he given up using Ecstasy?

"Various reasons. There's the long or the short answer. After twenty or so times, I've become rather disenamoured of ... I think I might be calming down ... becoming ... over the last few years ... I don't, I don't like the music ... all that ... its all clubby stuff. It's alright if you're in a club, but generally I just hate it. I've grown out of it I suppose. Like the pattern of drug use generally. Psychologically, to consume a drug takes so little effort. But for what? Just so much ... so much trickery! People feel better about themselves, and about the world, but it's an appalling trick. It's ... I get into a tremendously bad mood, actually, when you mention it! My memory's possibly blurred, because I was mixing E with alcohol ... It's actually a negative thing. People don't look at other people and recognise the bad points when they are doing E: life's supposed to feel great! But I doubt Ecstasy has any more potential to suppress all kinds of psychological stress and disturbances than anything else..."

Danny is now 25. When we originally spoke to him he was gradually reducing his use of Ecstasy. Now he's given up too. Why?

"Eh? No reason, just don't fancy it at all ... been and done. Because I'm not into it, I haven't actually sat down and thought about it, but I just don't. I think the time had come and I just got frightened. Maybe, the effects, the side effects it was giving me ... eventually later on in life, just enough, enough, and stop it. The last time I took it was two and a half years ago. It was okay, but that was it. I don't think there was anything that really I enjoyed. Just all my friends were doing it and I was doing it as well. We seemed to be all on the same wavelength at the time. That's probably why..."

Agnes, once a medium level Ecstasy user, still uses it, but she is still only 24 years old. Yet how often?

"Occasionally. I think you need it to feel you're taking part and be with everyone else ... in most clubs, anyway. I guess I still do it, take E, about

once a month. Although the E is terrible now, they just make you tired now. They're a lot milder. I used to think if I took them that they would disagree with me but I don't now. I take them and I probably feel all right. I don't feel that much different, just more awake, more alert..."

We asked her if she ever experienced any problems with Ecstasy:

"Just ... not blackouts it's just when you try to think back on the night there's probably the whole middle bit is missing. You remember going in and you remember leaving but the night ... it just goes so quickly. You try to remember it, and it's difficult. I don't drink that much, so it isn't that. I take four drinks, but not necessarily alcohol. It's probably just a combination of both. You feel fine at the time. But you don't know what's in them, the E. You find that all drugs do that though. Like speed did that as well. Speed years ago was just something totally different from what it is now. Occasionally you might get something good but it's not often. But it doesn't worry me, the quality or the price, I mean. No, I would probably still do the same. But just the half. One would floor me, wouldn't it? I think it's enough, I think it's just greedy, any more than that..."

Sharon, is also now 23, and felt much the same as Agnes. Sharon was a light user then, and she is a light user now:

"Yeah, I still do it. Just when I go to a club. You get in there ... really you need the drugs. Everybody is ... I don't know, I just still enjoy a wee half. I don't take any more than that. Once a month is enough for me. Can't afford it ... can't afford to go out more than that. It's too expensive. But it's just the drinks and that, and to get in and all that on top of that. So you're probably talking about £40–£50 a night out. Trouble is, the E is crap. Terrible. Just ... I don't know ... it's because I took, like recently I've took maybe one half of something and it's been like not that good, and then I've took ... maybe I took another half of another kind and they've maybe, I don't know, interacted, but I just don't think ... I would say that instead of giving me energy, it kind of made me more alert..."

Sharon also felt she was getting old:

"My vision's worse, and recently when I've took them for the whole night in the club was like parts were missing, and like the next day I

don't remember parts. I get memory blackouts ... yeah ... a lot. But these Eees, they're called 'Exhibitions' that we got a hold of a while ago, apparently they're full of Ketamine and that's ... eh it's meant to have all kinds of side effects. But, you drink as well. It might be a combination of it ... but I wouldnae say I was drunk, but if I had six drinks [that is, alcoholic ones, unaccompanied by drugs] I would normally remember the night. Do you know what I mean? I'd say it's the E that knocks me, I wouldn't say it knocks me for six either. I don't feel like really smacky or anything, I just feel ... your body feels normal and you can still dance and that, but you don't feel sociable and you can't be bothered talking and that. 'Cos your constantly waiting for this buzz that isn't happening. It's kind of putting me off now. I'm just like that, like at New Year ... I had some E at a club, and you're just cold and shivery, and you feel tired and I just wanted to go home. It just made me really tired, and I thought 'it's a waste of time! I've got to stop taking it.' ... I can take it a wee bit. I don't know ... I just presumed it was me because, like getting older, and getting used to them..."

Even Moira, who was a very heavy Ecstasy user when we spoke to her four years ago, is cutting down:

"I still take it on quite a regular basis ... em, it's just really if I'm out clubbing or if it's there, you know that's basically it. I would say I take it maybe once a month, less than before. I take it if I'm going out in the weekend. It's not because I can't handle it the way I could, but with me being travelling it's more difficult to come across ... so it was just basically that. Anyway, it was opportunity, as I say. I just couldn't get a hold of it me being up north of Scotland. I've been working away in hotels. Em ... it wasn't because I thought 'Oh it's time to give it a bye', you know. It's just a case of I couldn't get it. But I take a lot less than I did. I was 13 when I took my first E, and now I'm 23..."

On the face of it, this all seems rather remarkable, but there are no scientific grounds for imagining that these seven people are in any way typical. However, it is intriguing that they all gave the same three types of reasons when we asked them to explain their current attitude to Ecstasy. The first reason involved beliefs about the declining or changing quality of Ecstasy itself. First, Fraser. He told us that when he last had Ecstasy:

"...the quality had gone down. Certainly in the previous few years the quality was much better ... em ... I can't tell, but I think it was probably on the way down by then. I mean it was quite rapid and I might have been still going out reasonably regularly then I think, I can't remember. I'd have to go back to '89 when it started off. It's something like: it peaked in '91 and tailed off in '92, '93 but it was still going on up until mid-'96 I would say..."

Stuart went on about it at length:

"E is like most commodities. The quality goes down as the masses get into it more, so you're still getting a hit off it, but it's not like it really was before, you know? You might still get still some hit, you know? As a person who has tried quite a lot of drugs I notice the difference in qualities, and if you have something good you're not going to take something that might damage you in the future if you're not getting the quality compensation for it. I don't really know but I think it is pretty crap these days, from what other people have been saying. I mean, I know people that are taking about 4 a night now and they just sit down and they're not dancing. I mean, I was invited to an E party, a mad E party, and I was like 'yeah! let's go'! So you go there, and you're for a dance, and you've got your dancing shoes on and all that, so you're all ready, and you're in for a dance 'cos you know these hard core, you know these people that you met 5 years ago used to like have totally unbelievable parties ... with like, you know, you were there on the stage together, and it was like a story from start to finish right? And everything had it's place. So and these people are totally hard core right? And the music was hard core, so it was the business right? So they invite you to a party 4 years later, right? But the crux of the matter is everybody is sitting down, so I'm thinking maybe they haven't taken their drugs yet, so, eh, I made a few enquiries. I didn't have any drugs on me so I made a few enquiries ... not that I was wanting any E 'cos it was getting near Christmas, so I wanted coke, and I thought there might be a bit of coke on the go. But ... em, what happened was they had taken their drugs and the only thing available was this E, right? And they all know their drugs, so it's going to be the best type available on the market at that time. And I'm going 'how many have you taken?' and they're like that: 'three so far', and then in the morning they were like that 'at least four'. And like they were just sitting there, and like the music they were playing was just crap right? Shite techno! Shite crappy rubbish! Everybody that started in the

beginning as fit healthy dancer ... at the end of it, you've got people like just sitting gouching out ... and I'm like ... Nobody danced all night, we had to leave ... yeah, that was boring. And because everybody was on E they were in their own sort of wee bubble. They seemed to be having quite a good time sitting down, but they were sitting down! It was a sitting down party! So you couldn't actually interact with anybody. That happens quite a lot now..."

Later in the interview, he introduced a new element:

"Nowadays, people take Eees to go to the pub. You're taking E to go to the pub! People that I used to dance with will take an E to go to the pub! Just to sit and talk! They are now taking E, and going out and talking about football and things like that. That's the scene, that's the E scene, know what I mean? The whole dance scene has gone like that. I haven't found a good dance night for like absolutely ages, years. Yep, and it's not just an outlook I've got. Other dancers say the exact same. I'll go out with my dancing shoes and I swallow some hash, which as I knew years ago when I used to go dancing, that is a better ... that gives you a better buzz than what E does. That's the key, that's the key point. You've got to be healthy to get the benefits from it and what it means is that instead of putting you to sleep like, or if you take a big bit of hash you take a whitey 'cos you're out dancing ... your body isn't allowed to slow down, and the music is lifting you because of the psychedelic effect of the hash so as the music lifts you instead of you gouching. Your body loosens and just like bursts into life, through eating hash and you have like an excellent experience. Right so you don't have to do things like E or speed or acid, it's effective with a bit of hash, just eat it. Yep, and you don't have the come down. Your body is okay. It's pretty ... you get a right good buzz of it..."

Stuart had some Ecstasy a couple of months prior to interview, so he was probably better informed than most to comment on it:

"That was sort of, you probably call it peer pressure 'cos it was like out with the crowd to one of these so-called brilliant nights to a club. I should have known something was suspicious when I was at the door and the bouncers went and stopped the guy in front of us and found a bag of pills in his top pocket. But the pills were not E, right? The reason the guy had them in his top pocket was because they were legal. They were viagra right? Flipping viagra! Bright blue triangle things.

And ... eh ... the bouncer took it and they were like that 'what's this?'
And the guy was like, 'viagra' and they were like that: 'cannae fucking
take that in there: it's pills!' And he was like that: 'but its legal' and
they were like that 'but it's pills! You cannae take pills in, right? 'Cos
you might be selling them as E or something like that'. So they
confiscated them, but he was to get them back later. But I thought
'fucking head bangers! They need viagra! ... Is this the sort of place I
want to be in?' You don't need stuff like that ... eh ... I should have
clicked and worked that one out. Anyway, they were all taking E, and I
hadn't taken E for donkeys, right? So I was like that, 'okay, I'll have a
half and maybe it'll be good'. But the music was crap ... before, people
used to get fit by going out to the dancing, but you don't get fit people
at the dancing any more. They're all like dancing couch potatoes!
They're all like up going 'oh yeah yeah yeah' you know, hardly moving
... so I turn round and go 'this is absolute crap' and afterwards when
we meet up I go 'that was absolute crap'. Because I'd just taken a half.
Maybe if I'd taken more, you know?..."

Moira, once a very heavy user, had plenty of experience to rely on:

"Back then E tended to be a lot more, you know ... it would give you
a lot more get up and go. I find now it's like smackey ... physical. It's
more kind of ... you just want to sit like totally out of your head, you
know what I mean? Rather than like running about the dancing like
going 'Ooooh'! You want to be up giving it laldy[23]*! But in saying that*
you still got the smackey E back then. I would just say you can't get
hold of a bouncy one any more. Rather than having, you know, like
having a choice, if you want to put like that. It's not like that any
more. You just can't get it. As I was saying, my brother takes it now.
He never took it back then when I first took it – he was too young, but
he's 18 now but he's taking it, and I can see in him he doesn't get the
same like what I was. I don't know if that's because he's a different
person and it affects him differently, but I think it's basically it's what's
in it. ... The bouncy E, you know the ones I was talking about ...
you're like 'Oh I could love the world!' ... do you know what I mean?
You're like 'Who are you? I don't care, your're my pal'! You know
that wasn't just the E, that was the scene as well. The scene came along
at the same time. Do know what I think? You know like smackey E,
right? You can go like you just can't be bothered and your eyesight's
going like sort of jiggery like I call it ... like jiggery eyesight and you're
like 'Give me a wee while, and I'll sit and tune in' ... but see once I'm

*coming out of that, then I'm like 'Hey ho! Right, how are you doing?'
I think it's just like that initial sort of bang. Like my pals say it's like
banging you over the head with a baseball bat. Still, that's how it was
with me anyway..."*

She, too, felt she was ageing. She continued:

*"I still go clubbing but I don't go raving. There is a big difference.
Clubbing is a mixture of drinkers, drug-takers and all that, and the
music's different. Of course you get your rave clubs but they are dying
out. They stopped them all because there were these unlucky guys who
died, and it put rave clubs under a lot of pressure with the media and a
lot of pressure by the government and stuff like that so it's all died
away. I think it's not so much the drug itself, it's that the scene's gone. I
think the scene has gone more than the drug..."*

The second set of reasons related to the fact that many of their friends
had given up using Ecstasy. As Fraser put it:

*"Most of the people that I know that were involved in clubbing are no
longer participating in a regular basis and I think most of them have
stopped actually. Probably the quality would have something to do
with it but also things just get played out over a period of time. I think
it's just a natural falling away you know. The quality of the E was such
that the come down was heavy and that might have something to do
with it..."*

Stuart:

*"Em ... like there's quite a lot of friends that I've got that are still
taking it to quite a large degree, and I can see changes in the effect on
them. Em ... quite a lot of them have withdrawn into themselves and
really unfit looking they're all ... just sort of like acting suspicious ...
all like paranoia type thing, you know. All that sort of stuff and also
the actual hit any E that I have taken over the past 3 years just hasn't
got the same type of psychedelic experience..."*

We asked him why his friends had given up:

*"It's a combination of both age and the quality of the E. One of my
friends is going through this now. That's the problem. He's going*

through this crisis just now and the E aggravates it. I think there is a lot of people that keep taking it like all the sort of 30s generation, it's not happening to me, but it's like, I'm saying, it's happening to people. Apparently, see, that's another thing that's changed about E. Nobody vomits anymore on E. Before if you vomited that was a good E. Right if you vomited it was a good E ... that was the rush. You used to get a rush like injectors explain a rush. I've never done that, inject anything, but I can understand where they're coming from because you used to get a rush with E. It used to make your legs tremble. The muscles in your legs would jump about like a big elastic band. You would actually think that was happening. If you looked at it you couldn't see it but you could feel it. That was the energy rush you would get, right? And it would envelop you, and all of a sudden you would burst into the reality of what used to be an E world..."

He, too, felt that things had changed:

"It's not like that now, you don't get this effect of the drugs anymore, but that was why I started taking it. You would burst into a world where there would be a king and queen sitting in front of you ... that would be like two of your pals and they would be like extremely accommodating, you know and immediately you would be like them also. So you would get that at the start, and then you would have like projectile vomiting, right? You realised that was a bit unpleasant but you simply wiped yourself clean, and that was you. People would be like 'oh he's been sick, how are you feeling?' and you would be like 'oh, I'm feeling a lot better now' within maybe about 5 minutes you'd feel a lot better and that would be you. Other times, you would probably be falling asleep and having to consciously keep awake and like feeling crap 'cos you know you've got an E that's got something else in it and it's not an E. It really pisses you off 'cos you may have done yourself damage 'cos you don't know what you've taken. You can still move, but you feel really tired. Still, then it was just everybody you know, the crowd. Em, you were just part of a new entity that you were all part of but you were all connected to. There was no barriers ... no taboos..."

To Stuart's account, Danny added: *"I still go out on the clubbing scene, but I'm not aware of it. If they are [taking Ecstasy] I don't see it at all. My friends aren't taking E any more. None. Well, if any of them are, I'm not aware of it...".*

However, Moira's friends were still users: *"my friends are still doing it, and they love it, they are still going to this club, which is one of the few that are left. My friends from then are still taking E. A lot of them have got children now, or met someone who doesn't take it, and they think, 'I better not' … Em … but they'll still take it any opportunity they can…"*

A final set of reasons reflected personal maturation, although, of course, this is heavily linked to friends also growing up. Stuart first:

"I stopped at the good bit before it got bad! So I've stopped after that last one when I took a half one. I was like 'I'll only take it once every 15 years' or something like that, so you don't get a battering off it. And then you maybe wait another few years and by the time you're an old crusty you might as well take a few, you know. Anyway, yeah, I'm working more nowadays, much harder than when we last spoke. Well not so much harder but it's just that things have maybe pulled more together. The work I done then has paid off. It's been another goal to move me on, kind of thing. And another thing, em … I think during the last interview I did have the same partner and we're still together, so that's good…"

Richie was rather depressed about it all. He looked back on his Ecstasy using phase in a rather sad way:

"E users are false and superficial, and E sellers are superficial and false. I'm more into other drugs, and don't feel that E use had enhanced my way of thinking in the kind of way other drugs did, such as LSD. I even preferred heroin as a drug to E! I worked hard to fend off the superficial feelings I felt when on E and didn't like meeting people who were so affectionate to me when they didn't know me, and they were on E. As I said, I don't like the music scene and don't really go to clubs. My lifestyle has changed. I'm now working much harder than before and making my way up in my career. I've got more responsibilities than I did in the past. My life has changed into one where I want to concentrate on my career. Look, I still consume alcohol and tobacco, but I don't see myself as taking many other drugs. I don't see myself taking E again … although I don't agree with saying 'never' … I prefer to wait and see if one day I will take some. The last time I took E, I didn't enjoy it, and felt annoyed at myself for taking it. Some of my friends still take E, but I think they're stupid and I don't want to take part in it. It's a too superficial an experience…"

Danny was more cheerful:

"Don't ask me what the E scene is like now. I, could, couldn't really answer that because I don't know it anymore. Two, two and a half years ... it's a long time. I haven't changed, although I've a better job, a better position in my job so I don't think it's affected it at all ... I still socialise, yes, but I don't necessarily have the same friends. I mean, in those days I've seen a lot of people who thought they were your friends, were just your friends in club, you don't see them anymore, so it's like anything. All I do now, is eh, smoke marijuana from time to time. And alcohol, yeah. Tobacco. Just hash. Twice a week. Eh, just having a puff, I would say..."

For Agnes, money was the problem:

"But I'm talking as if I'm still clubbing! We go to pubs more, now. It's cheaper. I've got bills to pay! E is more for a night out. If you're going for a night out, it's combined with that. It's still happening, it's just a different generation are coming into it now. We're the old ones now ... on the way out!..."

This is something of a change for Agnes (she's now only 24) who, four years earlier, said that she *"wouldn't take it in a pub"*, as we saw in Chapter Three. Sharon, although only 23, also felt age creeping up on her:

"They're getting younger as I'm getting older! No, it's [the scene] quite druggy I'd say and quite fashiony. I can't say the atmosphere is as good though. You get a lot of people walking about in different steps. You know what I mean? You can get some people on coke. There are a lot of people walking about high as a kite on coke and then a lot of people, you know, like sitting out of their nut, on E, cannae even speak. So the night ... it's just full of different characters strutting about. It used to be more sociable. I think in general a lot of people were getting fed up with drugs. Do you know what I mean? 'Cos it's getting beyond a joke. You just go into a club and take drugs. And that's what you do. You get fed up going into a club and all you do when you talk to people it's ... you know, 'what are you doing to get out of your nut?' ... and that kind of conversation gets boring after a while..."

What were the other reasons for Sharon?

"It's the money. Anyway, I'm a lot busier now. Doing more. Life is generally busy. I go to pubs more. Em ... more responsibilities, I've bought a flat and got more to stay in for now. Do you know what I mean? Like I don't live with my parents ... and just live for the week-ends. So the E thing doesn't fit so much now. Except now and again. It's just for the night and clubs. I would not go to a party and have E. Do you know what I mean? You stick to hash and drink at a party ... it's fine but ... em. I probably do more speed than E now..."

For Moira, also now 23, it was much the same tale:

"It's different now. As I say, it's partly because of the music and I don't like that music. Aye, as I say I don't go out as much. The places that still do good rave music ... it's all like 17 year olds who go and all that. Maybe it's because I'm older and I'm not matured enough like all the rest of them at 23 years old but ... You know what I mean? I just don't go. If I went I could fit in ... I'm young in the head, so I suppose I could, but I just don't go. My best friend she takes, she likes the smackey E, she will take it sitting in the house, with her not wanting to go out all the time like me. I sit and reminisce a lot because I tell you, my raving years ... it will always be the best time of my life, the best times of my life, and I feel now that I couldn't recreate that, do you know what I mean? The world looks that wee bit different now that I'm older..."

WHERE ARE WE NOW?

To be honest, we don't know.

This isn't much of a conclusion for nearly a decade's work, but what else can we say? On the one hand, Ecstasy use has been associated with death, and some research into the effects of Ecstasy on the brain has indicated definite changes. On the other hand, it isn't known how Ecstasy figures in the causal chain which has led, for an unfortunate handful, to death. Neither is it known whether or not the changes picked up by brain scans are either damaging or permanent.

As well as this, we were – to all intents and purposes, unable to discover any major negative consequences of Ecstasy use after years of detailed quantitative analysis of the responses of the 229-strong large sample. Admittedly, self-ascribed "depression" appeared to be linked to Ecstasy use in the responses of the large sample, and in the testi-monies of the small group. Yet, when we looked at this in detail, involving psychiatric consultants who administered standardised professional tests, it emerged that this was more related to the use of other drugs – especially the benzodiazepines – than it has to Ecstasy use.

Herein lies part of our problem. Such is the spread of illegal drugs, and such is the relatively non-selective take-up of them by consumers, it is well nigh impossible to find respondents who just use one drug. They can tell us – they did tell us – what the effects of Ecstasy were (they had all occasionally tried it when they were not using anything else), but, given the number of different drugs that they had used, it was impossible for us to analyse their responses to other questions and thereafter definitively link these general responses (for example, that they felt "depressed") to their prior use of any one particular drug.

At the moment, after something of a roller-coaster decade, we seem to be almost back to where we were in the early 1990s. Then, when Ecstasy burst onto the scene, it seemed almost like the ideal drug for the nation's young: it didn't involve the use of tobacco, it dramatically reduced consumption of alcohol, it wasn't in any sense addictive, and it encouraged young people to involve themselves in the sort of strenuous physical activity that many older people had previously complained that they were denying themselves.

Some people (older ones, most of whom drink alcohol, some of whom smoke tobacco, and some of whom may once have taken and even still take illegal drugs) think that younger people should use no illegal drugs at all. But – to be practical and realistic – Ecstasy seemed the least dangerous of all substances about 10 years ago.

However, in the mid-90s, a bleaker picture seemed to emerge. For various reasons alcohol began to reappear on the rave scene; greedy club owners gained a reputation for restricting access to free water; long-term depression was predicted for a whole generation; and every year one or two clubbers died "from" Ecstasy.

The early 2000s? Some of the direst predictions from the early 1990s now look rather silly. Far from becoming the long-term depressed, those few that we have been following, and to whom we spoke again as recently as early 1999, have matured, moved on, bought property, started careers – in short, have moved away from the hectic scene of their earlier years, and without any apparent permanent negative effect.

Some did remember being depressed. Fraser, for example:

"I have felt depressed, definitely, towards the end of sessions of taking E, I would prepare myself for quite a heavy depression coming up for

*maybe 2 or 3 days after it ... you know it might not kick in just imme-
diately. The intensity of the depression could last ... I would say ...
maybe a day, and then it could drag on depending on the mental state
as well, but it could drag on for a few days before you got through it. I
think it was definitely chemically induced because I don't tend to have
depression and this was a serious thing. A couple of times where you
could almost you know, well not quite suicidal ... but really heavy
really really down ... I could still perform, but just a general mood
swing and a very negative one at that which I attributed that to ... I
suppose what goes up must come down! ... but then it wouldn't necessarily relate to the highness I felt when I was on E. You know the
depression could come and I would have a pretty normal night. I think
actually the message being that it really only works for so long ... certainly for this individual! You could say you get the message, hang up
the phone!..."*

But having given up, he added that he was now, *"very positive, and
just appreciating life for what it is."*

Even if they have left it, the scene is still there, or so they tell us, but
now populated by new entrants younger than themselves. Ecstasy use
has by no means passed: indeed, a recent official report on the state of
the drugs problem in the European Union indicates that Ecstasy use is
more widespread here than anywhere else.

To face this, drug research will need to improve its methods. Simply
counting Ecstasy users is not enough, nor is quizzing them about their
abnormalities, for they seem remarkably normal. Perhaps the biggest
issue raised by this research is the combination of a diversity of Ecstasy
using experiences, and occasional adverse effects, along with an
absence of any of the problems traditionally linked to drug use. For
Ecstasy does not seem to be associated with addiction, delinquency,
disorder or psychological disturbances of any dramatic kind.
Respondents reported feeling physically unwell in various ways and
sometimes feeling psychologically affected as well. It is unclear that
Ecstasy is entirely or even partly to blame.

We do need clear information about drug consumption, but given
the apparently huge variations of strength and purity between different tablets of, for example, Ecstasy, we also need some analytic
confirmation – perhaps by hair testing – of individual consumption.
At minimum this information would resolve the rumours that Ecstasy
is sometimes mixtures of other drugs, or is of widely varying
strength.

We also need increased clarity about drug mixing. Taking Moria as an example, 2 tablets of Ecstasy, several grams of amphetamine and half a bottle of vodka (which at approximately 15 units is more than the women's "safe" weekly allowance according to the British Medical Association) does not sound like a model of low-risk substance use, but we would be hard put to guess what risks, at what level, Moria was exposing herself to. As far as we are aware there is no research at all on whether or not taking all these chemicals in 24 hours is worse than taking them separately on different nights of the week. Multiple substance use appears to be the norm for the chemical generation, but we do not know enough about and it is not clear that users do either.

Critically, what we also need to know about is "risk", because this is what our drug users think about. We need to know how they calculate risks, how they deal with them. How unlikely events (a media published apparently Ecstasy-related death) affects their calculations and their behaviour, and how their risk evaluation behaviour changes over time. Crucially, what leads anybody to estimate the risk of using any drug as outweighing the benefits from so doing?

In return for asking them boring questions about this sort of calculus, we feel that it might be a sound idea to begin to give them the information that they need for their calculations. What impressed us, amongst other things, about our respondents in the various studies reported in this book, was the fact that they were all perfectly normal and unfailingly polite, co-operative and intelligent members of society. They live in a peer-world where drug taking is normal and, given the problems they feel that they face, understandable and, above all, rational. How can their needs be catered for?

It turns out, from the European Union report, that Ecstasy use here is slightly greater, perhaps surprisingly, than in the Netherlands, which has been operating the sort of sensible and tolerant health-oriented Ecstasy control policy whose only unfortunate characteristic is that some old people think it would increase Ecstasy use if applied here.

We have little to contribute to policy, over and above what our respondents tell us they want. One theme came through strongly – and sadly. What our respondents wanted to know, above anything else, was what are the "risks" of Ecstasy use? Sadly, because this, of course, was the one thing that we couldn't tell them. Not because we didn't want to – because we didn't know. Listen, for one last time, to Agnes, one of the small group:

"I don't know. I mean people are going to take it whether it's legal or not. So it might be a good thing if they did let it be legal then it would be controlled and then you would know what was going in it. That Leah Betts thing: it probably made me think like 'I'm not going to go overboard and take more than one'. I suppose you know the risk really deep down, you know. You know that it's killed people, and you know that you know it can kill people. You know there is a risk. It can dehydrate you, it could kill you. It can affect your brain as well, your thoughts. Whenever you read about it in the paper, same thing probably. You go 'oh God! I'm never going to take that again', and then you go out and take a half one..."

Yet, if we asked them, as we did occasionally, whether or not there was anything practical that could be done, some, like Willie who we quoted in at the start of this chapter, mentioned the "safe" table system which is in increasingly widespread operation in the Netherlands. Briefly, this is a facility provided in many clubs and raves. Purchased tablets can be taken to a table where experts conduct a brief chemical test which indicates, roughly, whether or not the tablet contains Ecstasy or amphetamines, or neither.

Researchers in the Netherlands do not believe that this harm-minimisation measure increases Ecstasy use, and so the idea has much, apparently, to recommend it. Risk analysts might disagree, and indeed, the evidence on risk compensation (motor-cyclists wearing crash helmets and car drivers wearing seat-belts all drive less safely than before these risk-reducing measures were enforced) makes this hard to deny. Testing tablets can tell if they contain pure MDMA or something else, but cannot tell the user if it is "safe" to take the tablet, only that they are taking risks with Ecstasy rather than with something else.

However, if backed by adequate research, the potential gains are huge. We would gain the confidence and trust of members of society who run the risk of being outlawed for being, for them, normal and rational. We would also gain the sort of vital information about tablet purity which could complement the forensic confirmation of drug consumption we recommended above for future drug research. The Dutch safe table experts collect and collate all the data they discover from testing tablets, and they forensically analyse ones handed to them that they haven't seen before. In turn, this allows them to broadcast warning messages when appropriate. Don't forget: most of our small group bemoaned the declining quality of Ecstasy – the successful Dutch experiment, if implemented here, could keep an eye on such things.

If research can begin to approach the sort of normal drug taking described in this book in the future instead as a type of risk taking behaviour (rather than from a criminological or health orientated perspective) it might be possible to focus more centrally on the nature of the decision making behaviour that lies at the heart of the process of initiation into, use of and abstinence from the use of various drugs.

As a start, we see much in the safe table idea, although (bearing in mind the difficult political position Britain is in when it comes to drug control: chiefly the ever-present need to "give the right message") it might be wiser to rename them (Our suggestion would be as "risk tables"). It also might be more scientific. It is not clear that someone is safer taking a tablet whose only active ingredient is MDMA than taking a tablet that contains, for example, amphetamine sulphate and LSD.

In documenting experiences on Ecstasy, this research has identified that we do not know enough about the risks of Ecstasy use, nor enough about the risks of mixing different substances. We are not, however, inviting a simple biomedical trawl for every problem associated with Ecstasy use ever. Incidence – how often problems occur – and prevalence – how often problems occur given the numbers of people that use – will be extremely important for Ecstasy. At the moment both incidence and prevalence of problems seem low.

What are the risks of Ecstasy use?[24]

These are still not clear, but the following are possible: First, collapse, even death has occurred. However, this is rare, compared to the number of times that people use Ecstasy. Far too rare, in fact, to find any cases of it in this study. Yet, feeling "unwell" during a dance event was very common, but it was not clear if there were any links between this experience and more extreme collapses and deaths. Given that dance events involve strenuous exercise and often taking mixtures of drugs and alcohol, much unwellness will have little or nothing to do with Ecstasy. For example, a commonly recognised risk of cannabis use, particularly with alcohol, is taking a "whitey" where the user goes very pale and feels sick, or is even sick. Alcohol alone can easily make people unwell also, as can opiates. If the incidence of unwellness, even collapse, perhaps even death, associated with alcohol and clubbing were documented, it is plausible that they would find a high incidence of such problems. Nonetheless it is worth considering the issues shown in Table 5.3.[25]

The second major concern is that Ecstasy causes depression. On the basis of this study, we can conclude that Ecstasy use is not associated

COLLAPSE, EVEN DEATH

Possible contributing causes, along with Ecstasy	Solutions and tentative safety advice
Overheating (hyperthermia).	Chill out regularly.
Clubs too hot.	Adequate air conditioning in clubs, or open air events.
Too little water (dehydration)	Drink water or soft drinks to quench thirst.
Too much dancing	Take breaks from dancing. At a really hot indoor rave, you could lose 6 pints of fluid in 6 hours.
Too much water.	Water does not reverse the effects of Ecstasy, it just prevents dehydration. It is best to sip water regularly rather than drink a large amount in one go.
Mixing with alcohol.	Don't drink alcohol with Ecstasy, not even drinks that seem to quench your thirst, like beer or alco-pops.
Mixing Ecstasy with other drugs	Mixing drugs can be dangerous. Some combinations can be deadly.
Taking multiple tablets of Ecstasy.	Don't take multiple tablets at once and don't prolong an Ecstasy session for too many hours. Remember that large people can consume more drugs than can small people.
Exhaustion, perhaps worsened by illness or stress.	Don't underestimate the physical demands of dancing. Ecstasy can perhaps make you over-dance without you noticing.
Unknown personal risk people collapse on first use. factors – a few	Whatever these are you don't necessarily know that you have them. Maybe they include: *Heart problems*, that make it risky to over-exercise. *Liver problems*, such as hepatitis or damage from heavy drinking, that prevents the liver metabolising drugs properly. *Respiratory problems*, including asthma and hay fever, that might make exercise difficult. *Neurological problems*; perhaps some people are better at regulating their body temperatures than others. The key point is that you don't necessarily know. **So, be careful on first use.**
Unknown situational factors – a few people collapse although they have used many times before.	Exhaustion may be one (see above). We don't know what others there are. Perhaps people happen to develop health problems. Perhaps Ecstasy progressively damages some people's brains more than others. Perhaps there is a "factor X" that we know nothing about.
You are taking a small, but potentially serious, risk every time you take Ecstasy.	**No one can guarantee that any of these precautions will be effective.**

Table 5.3

with long-lasting depression of a type that might require treatment. Two related risks are of Ecstasy causing a rebound depression some days after use, and of Ecstasy progressively damaging the serotonin systems of the brain, so that users become more prone to depression later in life. We will deal with that shortly. Let us first look at rebound depression, in Table 5.4. Because Ecstasy is so widely used, we must be careful not to make attribution errors about depression and Ecstasy. The prevalence of depression is above 10% in the population and the prevalence of Ecstasy use is also probably above 10%. Even if Ecstasy users are no more prone to depression than anyone else, about 10% of them are going to suffer depression during a year. It is thus tempting, but invalid, to blame Ecstasy for any noticed depression. Table 5.4. also suggests a number of reasons for midweek depression or low mood that are not specifically to do with Ecstasy.

The third area of concern is the long-term effects of use. This study could not address these, except for the small sample that we followed up. It is, however, interesting that so many of them had given up using Ecstasy by follow up, saying that they got less effect from Ecstasy than they used to and that the drug scene had changed. They often attributed the reduced effects to weaker Ecstasy, but tolerance and ageing are also likely explanations. Serotonin levels in the brain tend to reduce with age and may be depleted with Ecstasy use. If users have less serotonin available, then Ecstasy cannot have such powerful effects. Changes in the drug scene also suggests ageing to us. As clubs fill with younger people being silly – but probably no sillier than those we spoke to used to be – it can feel to them as if it is time to move on.

Nothing is yet certain about the long-term effects of Ecstasy, but the concern is that it may permanently affect the serotonin systems in the brain, making them function less well. With ageing, serotonin levels decrease also. In consequence, less efficient functioning might not show up until middle age or older. It is possible that these effects could include depression and some deficiencies of mental functioning similar to early dementia. If these effects occur at all, then we still have no idea how serious they will be in practice. It will also be difficult to tell unless future longitudinal research follows up their current users carefully.

DEPRESSION	
Possible contributing causes	**Comments, solutions and tentative safety advice**
Depleted serotonin for some days after Ecstasy use.	Don't take Ecstasy if already depressed – it may have less effect and may worsen depression afterwards. Depletion is probably dose-related, so don't take multiple tablets.
A psychological "let-down" after the pleasures of the weekend.	If you've had a great time then it is not surprising if you feel a bit flat by contrast during the week. Don't take more drugs to cheer yourself up.
Hangover from alcohol and maybe other drugs.	As we have seen, people often take substantial quantities of other things before, during and after Ecstasy. If you've been high for over 48 hours on different drugs, then it is not surprising that your body may need time to recover. Be more temperate over the weekend, if you don't want to feel bad later in the week, or need to be on top form at work on Monday.
Exhaustion	Two six to eight hour sessions of strenuous exercise can take a few days to recover from, even if you are reasonably fit. Don't dance way beyond your normal fitness level.

Table 5.4

NOTES

[23] To use all your energy/put your utmost into something.

[24] How Glaswegian Ecstasy users consider risk has been nicely documented by Shewan, D., Dalgarno, P. & Reith, G. in their article, "Perceived risk and risk reduction among ecstasy users: the role of drug, set, and setting", **International Journal of Drug Policy**, 2000, (10): 431–453.

[25] We have checked the latest leaflets available from the pre-eminent advice organisation (Lifeline, 101–103 Oldham Street, Manchester, M4 1LW; telephone: 0161–839 2054), but neither we nor they are responsible for the tentative advice given here.

Further Reading

Rather than give a huge list of articles, books, and so on about Ecstasy (although we have one) we thought it might be more useful if we recommended just what we felt was the best in each category. So, the best sources are, on:

- **The contemporary British drug scene**: Howard Parker, Judith Aldridge and Fiona Measham's *Illegal Leisure: The normalisation of adolescent recreational drug use*, Routledge, London, 1998.
- **General overview of Ecstasy**: the late Nicholas Saunders's *Ecstasy Reconsidered*, published by himself in 1997. A good alternative is Richard S. Cohen's *The Love Drug: Marching to the Beat of Ecstasy*, published in 1998 by the Haworth Medical Press, Binghampton, New York.
- **The chemistry of Ecstasy**: Alexander and Ann Shulgin's *PIHKAL*, Transform Press, Berkeley, California, 1991.
- **The debate on legalising Ecstasy**: Sheila Henderson's *Ecstasy: Case Unsolved*, Pandora Soap Box, HarperCollins, London, 1997. An alternative is Kevin Williamson's *Drugs and the party line*, Canongate, Edinburgh, 1997.
- **Dealing in Ecstasy**: Bernard O'Mahoney's *So this is ecstasy?*, Mainstream Publishing, London, 1997.
- **The cultural history of the rise of Ecstasy use**: Matthew Collin's *Altered state: The story of ecstasy culture and acid house*, Serpent's Tail Press, London, 1997.
- **Ethnographic study of Ecstasy use**: Jerome Beck and Marsha Rosenbaum's *Pursuit of Ecstasy*, State University of New York Press, Albany, 1994.
- **Risk**: John Adams's *Risk*, University College London Press, London, 1996.

APPENDIX
The Information Needs of
Ecstasy Users[26]

"Drug taking isn't a problem in society is it?"
"Nah, it's just been made one 'cos they won't educate us ..."

INTRODUCTION

On the understanding, back in 1994, that Ecstasy was in widespread use in Scotland, and that many harm reduction materials – chiefly leaflets – are available to Ecstasy users, the task was to assess whether or not the (mainly English) leaflets were appropriate to the needs and experiences of (mainly Scottish) Ecstasy users. Their needs were assessed by conducting focus group discussion with identifiably different groups of young Ecstasy users, and following these up, where appropriate, with individual tape-recorded interviews. Leaflets were culled from as many sources as possible, and 13 key representative ones – in the sense of reflecting the available range of leaflets as measured by size and format – formed the basis for discussion and interview. Some 38 young people took part in discussion groups, and 21 of these were interviewed individually thereafter. The 21 were selected on the basis either of being apparently communicative, or the reverse (on the expectation that they might open up out of a group context). Slightly under half of the 38 were female, and all were aged between 16 and 20 years. Their patterns of drug use, their frequency of attendance at raves, and so on, were all broadly similar to those of the large sample of 229 discussed in the main part of this book.

The sizes and composition of the discussion groups, and the number from each who were interviewed individually is given in Table A1. In 1994, preliminary analysis of types of Ecstasy users mentioned by those interviewed as part of our large sample indicated that there were two main types of user. Firstly, "casuals" – ill-educated impoverished temazepam users who have encountered Ecstasy and other dance drugs on the rave scene. Secondly, "clubbers" – educated middle-class users, who are either "yuppies" (with an employment income, often a heavy dance drug use pattern, whose drug of choice is cocaine) or "students" (lower income, lower dance drug use, whose drug of choice is amphetamine – which is much cheaper than cocaine). Discussion group members were accordingly selected to represent these types.

INDIVIDUAL VIEWS: THE FORM OF DRUG INFORMATION MESSAGES

To guide the interview in each case, each respondent was asked initially to complete three multiple questions on drug information sources and required drug information content. The responses of the 21 interviewees to questions relating to how much information each had received from each of 10 different information sources is given in Table A2. Respondents were asked to indicate for each source, whether they received "a lot", "a fair amount", "a little", or "none at all" from each source. We have subsequently scored each as 1 for ticking "a little", 2 for "a fair amount" and 3 for "a lot".

For this set of 16–20 year olds, friends and other young people were overall the most popular source of information, followed by leaflets and TV programmes, and, some way behind, by newspapers and

DISCUSSION GROUPS		
Group name	Group size	Interviewees
1 Mixed students	7	3
2 Female "yuppies"	5	4
3 Female "casuals"	8	3
4 Male "casuals"	8	4
5 Male "yuppies"	3	3
6 Mixed "clubbers"	7	4
	38	21

Table A1

SCORES FOR EACH INFORMATION SOURCE							
Group number	1	2	3	4	5	6	ALL
N interviewed from each	3	4	3	4	3	4	21
1 TV Ads	1	3	2	3	2	1	12
2 TV Programmes	4	7	4	4	4	8	31
3 School	4	1	1	5	–	5	16
4 Parents	2	1	1	1	1	–	6
5 Leaflets	4	4	8	6	2	8	32
6 Phone Lines	–	–	1	1	–	–	2
7 Newspapers	4	4	2	3	2	4	19
8 Posters/Billboards	3	3	5	4	2	4	21
9 Friends	9	7	8	6	4	13	47
10 Other young people	6	6	7	4	4	10	37
Maximum possible score	9	12	9	9	9	15	3

Table A2

posters. School was not much in favour, and parents and phone lines hardly favoured at all.

All were then asked to say which drug information source was "best", "second best" and "third best", and data is given in Table A3. Here, to generate a score, a vote of "best" scored 3, one of "second best" scored 2, and one of "third best" scored 1.

It can be seen that friends stand well out as the "best" source, followed (at some distance) by leaflets and TV programmes.

SCORES FOR EACH INFORMATION SOURCE AS "BEST" SOURCE							
Group number	1	2	3	4	5	6	ALL
N interviewed from each	3	4	3	4	3	4	21
1 TV Ads	–	–	–	1	–	–	1
2 TV Programmes	3	6	2	2	3	2	18
3 School	1	–	–	–	–	–	1
4 Parents	–	–	–	–	–	–	–
5 Leaflets	1	6	7	6	1	7	28
6 Phone Lines	–	–	–	–	–	–	–
7 Newspapers	2	–	–	3	4	–	9
8 Posters/Billboards	–	1	–	1	–	–	2
9 Friends	8	9	6	2	6	17	48
10 Other young people	3	1	3	–	4	3	14
Maximum possible score	18	23	18	18	18	29	124

Table A3

When consulted in more detail, the individual interviews are quiet revealing. **Television advertisements**, overall, didn't score very highly (only receiving 19% of the votes they could possibly have polled). In the main, when they were disliked, it was because they just gave unwanted warnings rather than desired information. Many had seen ads relating to AIDS, and, to a lesser extent, heroin – neither of which they felt was relevant to them – but none had seen ads relating to dance drugs, and wanted to reserve judgement until they had.

How about **television programmes**? They scored overall substantially better than television advertisements, receiving 49% of the votes that they could have polled. More than one recalled the famous heroin episode in the school soap, Grange Hill, and felt that it had scared them from using it, and others recalled documentaries on the subject that had impressed them. Others had seen both documentaries and debates on ecstasy, and while they found them informative, some had been embarrassed to watch in front of their parents.

School was not heavily supported as a medium for transmitting the sort of information on Ecstasy that these young people want, only receiving 25% of the votes it could have polled. Most could recall the obligatory school lecture by the head of their local drug squad, but very few remembered anything positive about it.

Parents scored very badly, only receiving 10% of the votes they could have polled. One main reason was consistently the view that parents were least likely to respond positively or helpfully to either the knowledge that one of their children was using drugs or to requests for information. All seem to be facing the same problem of the huge barrier placed between them as drug users, and them as their parent's darlings, by the media myths of the diabolical nature of all drugs. Even those who told their parents about some of their drug use, were often "gentle" with them, and held off telling the full story.

Leaflets, however, polled well, receiving 51% of the votes they could have polled. This may have been influenced by the fact that all had recently (and always prior to the individual interview) taken part in a discussion group where different leaflets were distributed for comment. Some thought that leaflets were good for beginners, but not so much use later on, and views were generally mixed as to leaflet content.

Phone lines polled worst of all, receiving only 3% of the votes they could have, at best, polled. Few thought them relevant to casual as opposed to problem users: however, they have a place even for normal users, as several recalled using phone lines to obtain leaflets.

Newspapers polled rather well at 30% of their possible vote, particularly as this group (if national statistical data are reliable) has only just started to read them, and especially as nobody has anything really positive to say about them. A rather different picture came across in the interviews. The feeling that newspapers carried a lot of "drug" (=junkie) news was shared, as was the feeling that it was hard to learn anything from such distorted, sensationalised and stereotyped coverage.

Posters and billboards polled slightly higher, at 33% of what they could, at maximum, have achieved, although, again, as with other forms of advertising, it was felt that the theme of posters is the "shock-horror" approach that so few actually appreciate.

Friends topped the poll, with a 75% success rate. Young people take drugs because their friends take drugs, and they take them with their friends when they take them. They believe their own experiences rather than media images, so when a media image contradicts an experience, they ignore the media image.

Other young people are also a popular source of information, polling 59% out of a possible 100%. "Other young people" is a category very close to "friends" (and is preferred for the same reasons). The particular utility of other young people is that they can extend one's information base outwith one's friendship circle.

In sum, none of the young people had seen any television advertisements about Ecstasy and most were charitable enough to withhold critical comment until they had. However, it was clear that straight information, rather than dire warnings, were what was felt to be needed. Television programmes – particularly non-fictional ones – are apparently more likely to have an effect on more educated young people, although even they can be put off by programmes that include anti-drug contributors as a way of creating debate or ensuring balance. Fictional portrayals (for example, the well known heroin user in Grange Hill) are memorable, and seem to have an effect of convincing some that heroin, in particular, is so bad that it should never be used. School is not believed to be an appropriate locale for the provision of the sort of information required (factual and non-moral). Instead, school is believed to be locked into the need to present the frightening preventative information. This is not to say that school might not be the best place to deliver information, of a different sort, which has been developed elsewhere.

Overall, it seems that parents will need far more educative input than their children before they are in (and are believed to be in) a position to listen, let alone help. Leaflets, especially if they are humorous, short, small, based on cartoons and produced by people with drug use experience, are welcome. Phonelines are believed to be of use either to people with particular problems, or to those who cannot get hold of leaflets any other way. Newspapers are not highly regarded as sources of useful information, but are believed to be a good source of routine "stories", and might function to warn people, although they are seen to concentrate much more on the (few) injectors than the (many) Ecstasy users. Most participants were aware of posters, but unimpressed by the content to the degree that they are disbelieved because of their warning "form" even by those with no direct experience of the drug itself. Overall, friends are by far the most trusted and widely believed source of information, because they are drug users, because they are friends, and because they are not seen to have any motive to lie. Which is, unhappily, how official sources are defined. Other young people function much like friends. However, although they might not be trusted quite so explicitly, they have the capacity to bring more information into the in-group.

INDIVIDUAL VIEWS: THE CONTENT OF DRUG INFORMATION MESSAGES

All 21 individual interviewees were then asked to rank each of 10 possible drug information "contents" in terms of whether they "strongly agree", "agree", "don't know", "disagree" or "strongly disagree" that each should be covered in drug education. As a rough and ready way of summarising, we have scored votes as "strongly agree" = 2, "agree" = 1, "don't know" = 0, "disagree" = –1; and "strongly disagree" = –2. Results are in Table A4.

The maximum possible score was 42 (strongly agreeing with all), and the minimum –42 (strongly disagreeing with all). Virtually nobody wants to be told where they can get drugs, which, amongst these respondents who are admitted drug users, indicates either complete

SCORES FOR EACH INFORMATION CONTENT							
Group number	1	2	3	4	5	6	ALL
N interviewed from each	3	4	3	4	3	4	21
1 Long term effects	5	7	4	3	5	9	33
2 Health risks	5	6	3	2	5	9	30
3 Help talk to parents	1	–	–1	–1	1	1	1
4 Help refuse drugs	3	1	–1	3	1	1	8
5 Help use drugs safely	4	6	4	2	3	10	29
6 Help talk to friends	1	5	3	–	3	7	19
7 What drugs look like	3	5	3	4	–	7	22
8 Where to buy drugs	–4	–4	–3	–2	–5	–2	20
9 Legal position	1	4	4	2	5	9	25
10 Side effects	3	1	3	–	4	3	14
Maximum possible score	6	8	6	6	6	10	42

Table A4

sureness about supply, or, more probably, a moral attitude not entirely in synchrony with personal behaviour. Being helped to talk parents, or empowered to refuse drugs are dismissed by most. Information on side effects, what drugs look like, and how one might talk to friends all receive some support, but not nearly as much as: information on legal position, how to use drugs safely, and the long term medical effects.

The individual interviews are again revealing. **Long term effects** seemed to be a worry for most members of all groups, and also the subject of considerable mythology. Desire for information on long term effects was the highest scoring content, with 33 votes out of a possible 42. One of the "mixed students", for example, told us, when asked about long term effects:

"I dunno … speed, I've heard speed wears down your bones… I just heard it recently, just a story about some guy who'd … he'd broke his leg, or something … just shattered, split completely… I'm not so sure … it just sounded like the effects could wear you down …"

Another believed an equally unlikely story about the effects of Ecstasy:

"These two guys who I knew … both had exactly the same thing, and that was their insides were absolutely completely wrecked … they were waking up every morning without fail, they'd go and vomit in the toilet. Their digestive system … their bowels were absolutely wrecked … "

"Purely from Ecstasy?"

"Well, this is it ... they didn't drink, they didn't smoke ... but they'd done Ecstasy twice a week to thrice a week for about 6 months, and I mean ..."

One of the "male yuppies" believed a similarly bizarre tale about Ecstasy:

"... when I was taking drugs, I mean, I knew that it certainly rots your teeth, and that used to really worry me ... and ... Ecstasy definitely gives you Parkinson's disease, which I've heard rumours... I don't know if that's true, but if that was definite, I think you'd kind of sit up and take note, albeit not much notice, but notice all the same ..."

Two of the "female yuppies" were more worried about schizophrenia:

"Well, the cases I've heard ... you can get schizophrenia, and paranoia ... and migraines came into it as well, like pains in the head, and stuff ... you're gonnie get paranoid all the time and it affects you in that sort of way and ... like, I've heard quite a lot with Ecstasy and things you can sort of lead to mental disorder, which really scares me ..."

"One of my friends ... this girl is, you know, schizophrenic through taking acid and she's only the same age as me, 20, and that's her [for the] rest of her life probably ... never work, and all the rest of it ... I thought that was a bit scary, quite scary, actually ..."

Part of the problem is that the current wave of synthetic dance drugs throws new substances on the social beach with such rapidity and frequency that there is rarely sufficient time for a folk lore encompassing likely effects, things to do, things to avoid, and so on, to build up before the next drug arrives. A "female casual" explains:

"Aye, wi' Ecstasy an' 'at ... they don't know what the long term effects are ... wi' acid or cannabis ... it's been around for a long time, but wi' Ecstasy, it's like a new drug, so it would worry me ..."

Health risks, of course, are not just long term, although responses here were much like those given in response to questions about long term effects. Scoring 30 of a possible 42, health risks were second only to long term effects in popularity. One "mixed student" appealed for honesty in information on health risks:

"I know that like taking speed over a long period of time is particularly bad for all sorts of parts of your body like your brain, your teeth, your weight, everything. I think it's the one thing … that rather… I think the problem with information before on drugs has been just plain and simple: 'Don't Take Them. They Are All Bad. Don't Take Them' … but I think if you said, 'Look, if you take this drug …' if people were actually honest in their leaflets and they said: 'Look, if you take speed once a month for the rest of your life, chances are nothing's going to happen to you'… But you should let people know that if you take speed every day, then it's going to affect your health and that is more likely, if you've got an all out thing saying 'Don't take it' … then somebody young, particularly somebody young and a bit stupid, is going to deliberately go: 'Right! I'm going to take it and see! I'm going to prove them wrong. I'm going to take that' … whereas, if you let somebody know that, 'Yeah, you can take it, it's not going to be a problem, but if you take it all the time' … then they are more likely to take it in moderation, I think …"

Rumour is as rife here as with long term effects. A "male yuppie":

"I was watching a programme … they'd given a monkey some E, I think, and like it had, it was given a kind of scan of the brain, or something like that, and like it had, it had a normal scan, and next, they scanned the monkey they'd given the E to, and the scan was perfectly normal on the left [side of the brain], but the one on the right, it'd like all the, a lot of brain cells had just totally disappeared, you know, well, so I mean, if people said it rots your brain power, or something like that, then that would worry me … or if it, I don't know, if it deteriorates your muscles, I think that would be a worry also …"

Information to enable individuals to **talk to their parents** isn't wanted at all, and scored only 1 out of a possible 42. The most consistent feeling was that parents needed to learn about drugs: not that drug users needed to learn how to talk to their parents. As one "female yuppie" put it:

"I doubt it [that talking to parents would be of any help] … if anybody did have a problem, or they were worried about anything … probably their parents are the last person they're ever going to go to … but I

think if your parents had just a wee bit of background, it might make it a wee bit easier, it might make them understand a wee bit better ..."

Parents are expected to overreact (and probably in the wrong direction). Three more "female yuppies":

"... your parents don't really know, like they know about it, an' that, but they don't see the other side of it, I think like they'd just panic a bit, and think that I was sort of gonnie turn into a junkie or something like that ..."

"... in my career, I'm doing quite well the now, right? Got a lot of ambition, and I've done a lot of shows, competitions and won things [she is a hairdresser] *... my Mum's quite proud that way, so I think it would shatter her illusions a wee bit if I started telling her that I took drugs quite often ..."*

"... they [parents] *don't know ... I mean, my Mum found cigarette papers and rolling tobacco in my bag, and said, 'Listen, if you can't afford to buy cigarettes, I'll give you the money' ... they haven't got a clue! ... they'll know a wee bit about it because they'll watch the things that are on at tea time, and the news, and they'll pick up wee bits here and there, like what happens at raves ... they'll know a little bit ... but apart from that, they couldnae tell you what it did to you, and why you shouldnae take it ... nothing like that ..."*

One "male casual" had talked to his mother about his drug use, but only partly:

"Aye, I talked to her before aboot drugs ..."

"Have you? How did that go down?"

"She just says, 'Never take E, man. Never' ... 'cos'a aw the things on the telly'n aw that, cause'a aw the people dyin' at Hangar 13'n aw that ..."

"Does she know you take drugs?"

"She knows I smoke hash, that's it ..."

One of the "mixed clubbers" didn't confide in her parents: they just found out. In her own words:

"... well, when I first started taking E, my Mum and Dad found out, right? And my Dad had taken things when he was younger, and stuff, and my Mum hadn't, and she started reading all the like Sunday Mail and all the rest of it, right? And I've had this wee poly bag with, like, all the little articles cut out, 'E KILLS ANOTHER', you know ... and it's just ... she was totally freaked out and really scared ..."

Another "mixed clubber" also found that the only bridge possible is parental drug use:

"I can [talk to her parents] now that I'm a bit older, and I can talk to my Dad more cause he's taken stuff ... but I just say to my Mum now 'I don't take it any more', 'cos that's easier for me, know what I mean? [laughs] ..."

Information empowering individuals to **refuse drugs** was again rejected by most, receiving only 8 out of a possible 42 votes. The better educated younger people tended to reject the idea, exclaiming that if accurate and honest information were available, people could choose what to do, and this might well include refusing some drugs. Just being taught to say "No" was seen to be naive and disempowering. One of the "mixed students" put it like this:

"I think if you've got somebody who knows that they don't want to go on a trip, or they don't want to be totally out of control, then they should have the information at their finger tips, where they can say, 'well, I know what that'll do' ... and you might think it's really good, but I wouldn't enjoy it, and that doesn't necessarily become a negative thing in a leaflet or anything. ... [you can go] ... 'Oh, this is brill', and he goes, 'Na, I'm not into that' ... then they can decide not to take it ..."

This was echoed by one of the "mixed clubbers". He said:

"I answered 'Don't Know' on the Help You Refuse Drugs [question] 'cos I don't think that's ... I disagree with that as being the thrust for drug education, but then I think that balanced information on drugs will help you refuse drugs ..."

Yet the less well educated did believe in pressure to take drugs, and felt that help to resist it might be a good idea, particularly for younger people, or people in early stages of their lifetime drug using career. One of the "female casuals" told us:

"Because ... the first time when I got offered an acid, like it was kinda 'Just take it' ... 'Just take it' ... an' like, I don't know because I was a wee bit, you know, younger, well, I was younger of course than I am now, but it was like if there's a lotta people'n like they're saying 'Just take it', 'Just take it' ... like the kinda thing I seemtae dae like a lottae the time, I just, I cannae say 'Naw', because I dae wantae try it, but I don't wantae try it, an' like they're slaggin' ye, so like ye go 'Right, I'll dae it'. It's peer pressure, and like a lottae people, just, they cannae say 'No', if somebody does say this, they'll dae it, an' like if there's a lottae them slaggin' them, then they don't wantae be the odd wan oot ..."

This feeling also emerged with the "male yuppies". One said:

"It's more of a peer thing, I think ... if your friends are all, for if your friends are taking it, then you feel kinda ... the pressure ... and they won't even be saying [anything] but you feel, to stay part of the group, you might have to take it just to sort of stay in with this group, or whatever... So, I mean, yeah, [people] should be helped to have a wee bit more willpower, maybe ..."

However, the provision of information to **help you use drugs safely** was welcomed, and received 29 votes out of a possible 42. Curiously, most had little to say on the subject other than wanting the information. One female "mixed clubber" said:

"Definitely... I mean something like if they could have at raves, you know, in big like flashing signs that flash all the time saying 'Remember to Drink Water', or something like that, you know, or, 'Don't Take ... Don't get completely steaming and then go out and take an E, because it might have barbiturates in it, and that with bevvy can kill you' ... and stuff like that ..."

The relative absence of safe using information on the Glaswegian (as opposed to the Mancunian) dance scene probably accounts for the relative inability of our Ecstasy users to articulate the precise nature of desired messages.

Information to **help you talk about drugs with your friends** was cautiously welcomed with 19 votes out of a possible 42. The reasons were mixed. One was advanced by one of the "mixed students". He said:

"There's bound to be somebody out there with their group of friends who likes a certain drug, but knows they would just get hassle from friends if their friends found out they took it ..."

However, occasionally the problem might be with the friend rather than with oneself. One of the "female yuppies":

"Even sometimes when you're talking with your friends, you still hold back a wee bit like sometimes you don't want to turn around and say something, you're all probably thinking it, but you don't want them thinking that you're more involved than you actually are, sometimes you sort of try and just say like I can go out at weekends and I wouldn't take anything, fine. But it's not as easy as that sometimes ... if I stay in, I'm fine. If I'm out, I can't go out and just not take any-thing... I'd find that hard, I didn't really want my friends ... 'cos I thought they'd think 'She's getting worse' ... but I spoke to them ... and, now, I'm staying in a wee bit more ..."

Most agreed with the sentiment (i.e., that one should talk to one's friends) but didn't see that they should be actually helped to do so (one of the "male yuppies" put it: *"it's just natural, I mean, you don't need to read about that at all, it's just going to happen ... it's just kind of, it's just natural"*). Others pointed out that you should tell your friends what you have taken, so that if anything goes wrong, at least there won't be doubt about the possible cause.

Knowing **what drugs look like** was also welcomed, now with 22 votes from a possible 42. Most agreed that a major problem was not knowing for sure what drug is being ingested, and worse, that a drug has been paid for but only a non-psychoactive product supplied. A "mixed student":

"... [you need such information] so you don't end up with the wrong rubbish like I did when I went to take E, and ended up with ketamine. I suppose E comes in that many forms, that you can't really tell. It [knowing what drugs look like] also stops you getting ripped off,

which is a good one as well 'cos it is very easy to get diddled when you're buying drugs ... its useful to know what they look like ..."

Two "male casuals" expressed much the same sentiments in their own way:

"Aye ... 'cos somebody could gie ye like say 'Aye, here's an E' or something, an' it isnae wan. They've gave you somethin' a pure duff, man, an' you don't know what it looks like an' don't know any better 'an take it, and don't know what could happen, man ..."

"'Cos you don't know whit you'd be takin', could be anythin', you could be, if you're payin' money, you could be gettin' bumped [ripped off] or something, know, if you don't know what they look like, I mean, you could be gettin' bumped ..."

A "male yuppie" echoed these views:

"Yeah, oh definitely, 'cos, I mean, people could take anything, I mean there's so much crap out there, I mean dealers will just shift anything they can, sometimes you get ketamine selling for E, and speed for heroin ... there's just so much crap in drugs ..."

Perhaps surprisingly, information on **where to buy drugs** received only negative support, with –20 votes out of a possible total of 42. This only received limited support if drugs were legalised. First a "mixed student" and then a "mixed clubber":

"It's probably not a good idea, people find out for themselves you know. I suppose that would be ... if it ever came to the point where things were legalised to a certain extent and that would be useful, but if it comes to the stage of saying, 'Well, if you go down to the bridge under Central Station, you'll meet a guy in a brown mac, and he'll sell you some speed,' it's a bit bad ..."

"I'm not quite sure what that question was meant to mean, 'cos ... I mean, if it was legal, then everyone would know because the people would advertise, and if it's illegal you can't tell people where to buy drugs because you're putting people at risk ..."

One of the "male yuppies" added:

"That's promoting it, telling you where to get it. You don't want them to know. Makes it easy for them to try it, I mean there's kids'll come up to you, and go, 'can you give us a bit of hash?' 'get us a bit of hash', and you're like that: 'No way!' ... people are going to find out anyway, so you shouldn't [tell them]... I think if you were, it's almost as if you are condoning the use of drugs ... just wouldn't be realistic at all ..."

Information on individual's **rights and the legal position on drugs** was welcomed, and received 25 votes out of a possible 42. There was almost universal support for knowledge here, particularly given the anomalous (for them) legal scheduling of Ecstasy in the same class as heroin. Two "female casuals" told us about their fears relating to drug use in public:

"... it's always good to know when the polis dig you up, or if you're smoking a joint, or whatever, man, they pull you up, you should always know what you're gonnie dae, what you're allowed to dae, if they start pushin' you aboot or anything ..."

"... because if you get caught wi' somethin' an' you don't know what's gonnie happen to ye, of course you're gonnie worry an' like that, 'Oh, I don't know what's gonnie happen to me!' ..."

Two "male yuppies" put it this way:

"Yeah, 'cos if you know what could happen to you for getting caught in possession of three E, you don't carry three, you're not gonnie do it ... should just tell you what'll happen to you if you're caught with them... I mean, it puts the shits up me if you're walking about a club and you've got two E in your hand, and you go looking for your friend, cause when you buy off your dealer, you're gonnie get done just as bad as him ..."

"Ecstasy does have quite a heavy fine, even, I think if you're caught with two, you can be put in jail for 7 years or something!... People should, yeah, people should know what's gonnie happen if you're caught ..."

Finally, one of the "mixed clubbers" put the problem in perspective:

"... people are going to come to more harm from being shoved away for doing drugs than they are by doing drugs. So the most dangerous part of drugs is the fact that you might get put in prison ..."

Finally, what about information relating to the **side effects** of drugs? Here, only cautious support, at 14 votes out of a possible 42, although a study of the transcripts revealed that there was some confusion as to what "side effects" actually were, and how to distinguish them from "negative effects" and "individual effects", and from "health risks" and "long term effects".

In sum, there is considerable ignorance coupled to considerable apprehension about the long-term effects of Ecstasy. It is ironic that the very area that users are most concerned about is also the very area that medical, or other, science is least able to help with information. There is a strong desire to be accurately and honestly informed about health risks. The level of misinformation currently held is worrying, and the desire for information is certainly matched by need. Users don't say that they want to talk to their parents, but they certainly, in the main, are not able to. Their feeling is that it is their parents who need educating: not themselves. Although not heavily voted for, most interviewees did seem to support the idea of helping individuals to refuse drugs. If implemented, perhaps this might best be targeted to the younger, less well educated groups and for two reasons. One, younger individuals are less likely to be users, and thus not entirely unreceptive to advice not to start. Two, less well educated individuals might benefit more from being empowered to say "no".

Most would like to see the provision of information to assist the safe use of drugs, but few can articulate directly or clearly what that information should be. These young people thought they should confide in their friends (for social, and for perhaps medical reasons), and that there were occasional barriers to doing this fully. Most felt that these would be naturally overcome, rather than overcome using specific situation handling skill acquisition. Overall, these young people supported the idea of information enabling more efficient identification of substances, but in so doing identified a deeper problem (that people just don't know what is in the drug they are taking even if a tablet does "look like", e.g., Ecstasy) which will not be resolved by more information on what drugs "look like". They take a surprisingly lofty moral stance over being told where to buy drugs. Their collective aversion to advertising the source of supply may reflect their own assuredness in being able to buy at will, but more probably reflects their unease at effective promotion of drug use (to possibly even younger people) under the currently unsafe circumstances in which users are obliged to use. Overall, there is a strong – even bitter – feeling that people should be aware of both their rights, and the legal situation with different drugs. With side effects, these young people reiterate their beliefs that any and all knowledge about the effects of different drugs should be provided honestly and openly to those who use them.

GROUP DISCUSSION: EXISTING LEAFLETS

The evidence collected so far has uniformly and consistently pointed to the need for more information, for honest and accurate information, and for information, at this stage, disseminated in leaflet form. Friends and other young people are the most trusted sources of information, but this seems to be not least because existing written materials are the wrong size (too big), the wrong type (not always in colour), are in the wrong form (too much writing), take the wrong tone (humourless) give the least useful information (don't take drugs), and are compiled by those least able to gain credibility with drug users (i.e., by non drug users).

The discussion groups focussed, apart from some introductory scene-setting discussions relating to the types of drugs that participants use and in what settings, and where they traditionally have received information from, exclusively upon leaflets. First we summarise group feelings on the 13 key leaflets they were shown.

Existing Leaflets

1. Lifeline's Big Blue Book of Dance Drugs (a 16-page large sized colour magasine which describes each commonly used illegal drug with a mixture of cartoons and text

One of the "mixed students" commented that, "… *that one, yeah, but this is quite good 'cos there's lots of pictures to keep you going along the way …*", and one of the "female yuppies" had an idea where it might best be placed: "… *should have them in doctor's waiting rooms … 'cos you've always got to sit for half an hour anyway, so you would read it …*".

However, another "female casual" said: "… *dead dull and boring, in't they* [i.e., usual leaflets]? … *just looking at that big book, it looks as if you'd sit and take time and sit and read a chunk …*", and one of the "mixed clubbers" said: "… *well, I've read the first page, right, an' it's really good, I really like the bit that says it's comparing like illegal drugs to alcohol an' its saying, you know, like the way the media put across is like if you take drugs, you're gonna die in the drugs addiction death bit but then its got the cartoon at the bottom saying you know the alcohol ... that's a good message to get across ...".*

2. Lifeline's Too Damn Hot (a medium sized monocolour tryptich leaflet mixing cartoons and text):

One of the female "mixed students" thought that leaflets this size would be good in pubs and clubs: *"... if you were sitting waiting for somebody to come back from the bar or something, and they [leaflets] were sitting around, you'd probably pick them up and have a look ...",* although another "mixed student" commented that *"... it would be tough to put the ones that are a couple of pages thick into a club ...".*

A "female yuppie" remarked that: *"... this just reminds me of myself [laughs]... D'you know what it says? It's a wee thingy, cartoon, in it, it says, 'Pete and Lisa are on one [E] at the club. 'Why is it when she sweats she looks sexy, but I just look as if I've pissed myself?' ...",* and it was liked by another three "female yuppies". The first said: *"... they're saying here, on this, there's a wee bitty guy saying 'You're trying to tell me it wasn't E that killed those casuals, it was heat stroke' ... an' then it shows you the dealer, and he's gobbed hundreds of E, and he's safe, and everybody goes like that, 'how come he's ...?' ... he's never dancing, he just stands there, so he can afford to take them, he's drinking water as well. ... Then it shows the ... saying 'here! ... that means that deaths from E are avoidable' ...".*

And the second added: *"... it's funny the E starts to take effect, then its his thoughts ... it's like that, he's lovely, you're lovely, everybody's lovely. That's really funny as well. 'E reached the parts that other drugs can't, but this didn't bother Pete, he just wants to hug everybody'... and it shows you how his penis has shrunk [giggles] ...".*

A final "female yuppie" told us: *"... That one! I like that! ... It's got humour as well, so you'll read the whole lot, but at the same time you're laughing, but you're taking it in, 'cos they're quite clever this way, they're making bits funny right? ... and then you get to another bit an' its serious ... it just goes 'Ooooh!', an' then you go to another bit, an' that, and they keep doing that, so you remember all the serious bits that they want to get across ...".*

"Casuals" liked it too. One of the "female casuals" said: *"... Aye, they're brilliant, have you read they ones? ... you would read them, an' you'd be gettin' information withoot even knowin' it, d'you know what I mean? It's just a wee cartoon ..."*. And one of the "male casuals" added: *"... Aw them, aw them are good, good wee stories in them'n aw that, good wee stories... That gies ye an idea what happens when you take the drugs'n aw that, what the precautions to take'n aw that'n aw ..."*.

One of the "mixed clubbers" – one of the few to comment from that group – claimed: *"... I've seen that one before ... thought it was quite humorous that one ... they'll know the common names which it gives in there and it also gives in there effects, and it tells you not to mix any alcohol with the drugs, and things like that, and getting dehydrated so that's telling youngsters like what it does, how to prevent like accidents happening, like trying to tell them how to take it in a safe way, and the form that it's in is easier to give out as a flyer in a nightclub ..."*.

3. Tollcross Drug Information Group's Emma E Head (a 4 side medium sized colour leaflet):

One of the "female casuals" said: *"... any place where young folk are hingin' aboot ... you're better havin' them in youth groups'n stuff like that ... or Emma E Head at raves or whatever, like ootside maybe, a wee stall wi' somebody giein' them oot 'cos you'll always like shove it in yer pocket and read it later if it's attractive ... 'Oh, that's a good laugh' ... have a good laugh wi' yer pal, you'd read it, d'you know what I mean? ... you wilnae just throw it away if it's funny'n ... aw. If it's somethin' pure borin', with hunners'a [words of] writin' on it, and you're just going intae a rave, it'll get tossed ..."*.

Another "female casual" said: *"... most of the leaflets in here [youth club] are no' like leaflets you're gonnie pick up from like say know how a Health Centre or something like that, they actually know how, like the ones wi' Emma E Head'n acid that it's like telling you about a bad trip'n that ... it's no' really don't dae this an' don't dae that, because I honestly don't think like if people's wantin' information they're no' wantin' tae read a book that says drugs dae this tae ye and drugs dae that tae ye ..."*.

4. Liverpool's HIT card on Poppers (size of a large postcard with pictures of typical bottles on one side, and information about effects, price, etc . . on the other):

One of the "male casuals" said: "*... that one's a good one I'n't it? ... poppers arenae like LSD or anythin' ... but they're just ... 'n aw that ...* [reading] *... 'use tends to be limited to certain situations, mainly the dance club scene where they're most used to enhance the effects of other ... LSD'... What does that mean? Like they're like acid'n aw that? It's no' because its no' ...*".

However, the "mixed clubbers" weren't so impressed. One remarked: "*. . What are they designed for? And where are you supposed to be getting them from? ... they are very soberly presented, you know what I mean? ...* [maybe they should be] *... in health centres, or something ...*".

5. Recreate's Acid Head (size of a postcard with a cartoon picture of somebody on LSD on one side, and information about effects, etc . . in a fake "Scottish" patois on the other):

One of the "female yuppies" said (of the companion card, Jelly Head): "*. . that one's good ... it's telling you what sort of class of drug it is and it's got a phone number ... it's telling you what it does to you, what not to do, and stuff ...* [the picture is] *. . quite good, but it looks more like a monster, maybe that's what you're meant to look like wi' jelly... I mean like the eyes are good, they're bloodshot an' red ... pupils are big, eyelids are dropped... 'If you want to find oot mair'... I think it's quite funny, it's dead serious, then it goes . . 'If you want to find oot mair' ...*".

One of the "female casuals" said: "*... there's no' too much, there's no' too little writin' on it, there's no' too much ...*", and another "female casual" added: "*... I like the way its a postcard'n all so that know how you'd send it tae somebody for a laugh or somethin', and that would be, I think that's their idea ... kinda' cause it's a postcard, you would send it tae somebody an' that information is on it ...*". A third "female casual" chipped in: "*... think the wee cards are good ... they're good, I like them postcard things ... like the postcards'n that, think that's good'n all 'cos it makes you read the back ae it ...*".

One of the "mixed clubbers" said: *"... that acid one doesn't tell you nothing ... the writing's crap ...".*

6. Manchester's Lifeline's Snidey E (a monocolour 9 page pocket sized booklet which is mostly text with a few illustrations):

One of the "female casuals" said:

"Naw, see that's black and white ..."

"Right, you didn't even pick it up because it was black and white?"

"... naw, cause aw the rest of them were aw bright'n looked mair interestin' ... that's pure crap, see that one? That is pure crap that, man ... pure boring. I read that actually, so I did ... boring and it's pure... You'd need tae lie in yer bed or somethin', man, try as get tae sleep wi' aw they ones ...".

7. Manchester's Lifeline's Ecstasy and Eve (another small, but this time coloured booklet with 5 pages of text and no illustration):

This one received bad reviews all round. One of the "mixed students" commented that, *"... I think this one's terrible ... because there's a whole load of small writing all about it, and then it's got 2 single lines ...",* and another "mixed student" added: *"... yeah, I got bored reading that ...".*

In another group, one of the "female casuals" said: *"... that one's dead ... too much readin' in it, so there is ...",* and another "female casual" backed her up: *"... I don't like this one... I think that's crap, that one 'The Lifeline Project has been producing information about Ecstasy for over five years' ... you could put that at the end, or somethin', or even just at the back, or somethin... Like see, if you were gonnie dae a project or somethin' like that for school, or whatever, then if you've got them, then I suppose that would come in really handy, 'cos it's got hundreds'a information ... but if you're just, if you're gonnie be coming oot the dancin', or whatever'n people's handin' ye big booklets, ye'd be like that, 'it's awright' ...".*

8. Manchester's Lifeline's Hot! Hot! Hot! (laminated postcard with a cartoon of people dancing in very hot conditions on one side, and advice to drink fluids and stay cool on the other):

One of the "mixed students" commented that, "... *these ones are just like one sheet ... are great ... like you see the picture, it attracts you, and you just turn it over, and its just got like a little paragraph, absolutely... If these were out in a club, I wouldn't pick up the ones that you had to flip through, you know, like 3 or 4 pages, of like, just text, but these ones like ... these are really good ...*".

Another "mixed student" added: "... *the smaller ones probably would be easier to put in a club, but it's gonna be difficult to put any kind of information in a club, you know ...*", and a third "mixed student" said: "... *see, the thing is, when you go to a club, you've decided before you go whether you're going to take something* [drug], *so what would be good would be if you had them leaflets somewhere where you could get the general health information about it ... so help you make a decision, and then when you're in the club ... not having any morals about it ... but just saying what to do ...*".

One of the "female yuppies" said: ". . *I like these wee ones ...*", as did another "female yuppie": ". .*These wee things are good, the Lifeline ones, 'cos it says about acid, remember, watch who you take it with, and where you take it an' you should be relaxed with people you trust and every-thing, and if things go wrong somebody gets a bad trip, try to relax them, take them for a walk or something. If you didn't know any of that, and you took acid, you could think, 'Och! I'll just take it an' go to the pic-tures', or 'I'll just take it at 8 o'clock' ...*". A third explained why: "... *see if you make it fun, man, it sticks in your mind ...*".

One of the "male casuals" said: "... *they ones there are good, they ones are good, they ones ...*", and he was backed up by one of the "mixed clubbers" from another group: "... *these wee ones are really good, 'cos everything it's saying is just bang on, d'you know what I mean? ... it's not saying stay away from ... it's telling you exactly what happens when ... and it's telling you, I mean obviously if you've taken it, you've made a conscious decision that you're taking it yourself, and it's just letting you know what to do on the drug. Obviously, these people have taken it, they know what they're talking about an' it's really good and its really funny as well, do you know what I mean? ...*".

9. Manchester's Lifeline's What's That? What's That? (another laminated colour postcard with two cartoon characters discussing adulterated tablets on one side, and a guide to interpreting which effects mean which drugs on the other):

One of the "mixed students" commented that, *"... I think they should have ones like this in clubs cause that is, you know, you can have quite a lot of information on there and it doesn't look stupid to pick up and it looks a bit like a flyer, not with the cartoons, but that sort of size, you know ..."*. Another "mixed student" imaginatively suggested that this sort of information could be built commercially into the commercial structure of the organisation of the club:

"I think the thing about those little flyers ... d'you know how like some clubs [give you] like a little ticket pass thing to get in and out ... if you're going out the door and come back in you need it, if you had, like, that information on the back of like their flyer, then maybe you're gonna keep it in you pocket, then you'll take it, you'll stick it in your pocket cause you need it if you want to go out and come back in again. Next day, when you empty your pockets or if you're sitting on a bus doing nothing, you might look at it ...".

From the "female yuppies" group, one said: *"... I don't think it's that funny ... but see, when you look at the faces and stuff, and their actions and what they're doing, and what it tells you on the back, I think it's really good ..."*. This found support elsewhere, too, with one of the "mixed clubbers" who commented: *"... they're definitely the best, 'cause they're not ... because they're making a joke out of it ... it's readable while being informative ... they're not scaremongering ... people aren't just going to sort of leave half way through and chuck it away, you know ..."*.

10. Liverpool's HIT's 3D What is a Drug? (a 3-D faint colour postcard issued with 3-D glasses with a picture of some drugs on one side, and some basic harm minimisation advice on the other):

One of the "male casuals" said: *"... that one's good for trippin', man ... fuckin' hamburger things or somethin' ..."* [two characters, called Harry and Hatty, on the card do, it has to be said, look like hamburgers].

One of the "mixed clubbers" said: *"... It doesn't ... it doesn't address it at all ... that should be a different format ... most of them don't address the issue …".* Another "mixed clubber" added: *"… they're funny …".*

11. Bridge Project's Your Guide to Dance Drugs (a monocolour tryptich with descriptions of Ecstasy, amphetamines and LSD, and some basic harm minimisation advice):

One of the "female yuppies" said: *"… I don't know if it's just me but … it wouldn't* [catch my eye] *… it's no' highlighted or anything important, apart from that …".*

A "female casual" put it pithily: *"… Just tells you no' ae take it, an' aw that, depressing … naebody's gonnie look at that … see, if they just had a bitta colour or somethin' … you're coming oot a rave, and they're giein you that, just throw it away … if you were goin' intae a rave, and they gie you that, you just throw it away …".*

12. Greater Glasgow Health Board's sparkly circle (a circular piece of card with sparkles on one side and minimum dance drug advice on the other):

One of the "male casuals" said: *"… I've got one of them in ma hoose … aye, it's a steel one, it's got a wee disk, you go like that, and spin it roon, an it aw kinda comes up … acid, brilliant, man …".* Although one of the "mixed clubbers" disagreed: *"… it's a good design if you're wanting this type of people to pick things up … don't give this to someone that's off their head, man, 'cos it would just fuck them up … imagine getting that on acid … that is the worst thing you could give to someone … well, to be completely honest, that's gonna blow your credibility altogether, giving that out …".*

13. Crew 2000's DUNT (a monochrome medium sized leaflet with cartoons – in "Scottish", and two pages of fairly dense text on drug use):

The only comment we got was from one of the "male casuals" who said: *"… Like that … good wee stories in them'n that … the colours are borin' …".*

Future Leaflets

No one publication is universally preferred, but the Lifeline materials are definitely seen overall as the ones that young people relate to most.

There seems to be a role for at least three different sizes of publication: magasine size, A5 leaflet size and small postcard size. Colour is definitely in. There is some ambivalence about whether or not they should be in standard English, and this will probably be best resolved by producing different products for different target groups. A cartoon style is almost universally preferred. As for content, straight information preferred over warning messages; humour preferred to seriousness; safe using advice is preferred to non-using advice; the choice between information from friends and officialdom is harder to make.

Different products should be placed in different locations, but the number of locations should spread from the current drug agencies to also include: schools, shops, cafes, clubs and raves. There are indications that for 16–20 year olds, magasines (like the Big Blue Book) might find an interested audience in GP waiting rooms, health centres and schools. A5 size leaflets (such as Peanut Pete and Emma E Head) will be most acceptable in drug agencies and youth clubs. Small glossy (because of the heat) postcard "info bites" would find an appreciative audience if distributed to those leaving raves and clubs, and if slipped into mainstream magasines and CDs.

Very generally, for this group of young Ecstasy users, leaflets are broadly believed to be the best form of information delivery. They agree that all leaflet type materials should be colourful, humorous, and eye-catching. They should stress harm minimisation rather than drug use prevention, should be peer developed, and they should give straightforward factual information. Pictures are more powerful than words.

Different materials should be produced for different socio-economic groups. Some of our interviewees had University degrees, others could barely write their names. It is absurd to imagine that one product will find its way to both groups. We feel that there are two main groups: "casuals" and "yuppies/clubbers". Within each, there are drug using initiates and experienced drug users. Both of these, too, need different materials. A fifth group is parents. Participants felt that it was this group which was most in need of drug education. A sixth group is the 5–9 year olds, to whom attention should turn soon.

NOTES

[26] In 1994, Jason Ditton was commissioned by the Health Education Board for Scotland to conduct a 5-month enquiry into the information needs of young dance drug users. This appendix is excerpted from the final report to HEBS, which was authored by Jason Ditton, Furzana Khan, Emma Short and Lesley Henderson.

Index

abstinence, from Ecstasy, 102–108
acid, *see* LSD
acid house, 111
    see also clubbing and also rave
      aspects
activities, non-drug, 95–6
"adam", 1
"adam and eve", 40
adulterated tablets, 4, 22
age, 4–5, 7, 19, 101
ageing, 136
aggression, 67–70
AIDS, 144
air conditioning, 135
alcohol, 10–18, 21, 45, 54, 57, 61,
    66–8, 71–2, 74–80, 83, 86–9, 99,
    107, 112, 117, 119–21, 127–8, 130,
    132, 134–5, 137, 158–9
"amber", 40
amphetamines ("speed"), 1, 3, 9–18,
    21, 23, 39, 47, 53–4, 77–9, 86–9,
    106, 117, 120, 123, 129, 132–3,
    147, 149, 164
amphetamine sulphate, 134
"Amsterdammer", 40
anti-depressants, 42
anxiety, 78, 116
appetite, 99
    loss of, 100
asthma, 135

B52s, 40
"banana split", 40
"bayer", 40

"bee bops", 40
benzodiazepines, 86–9, 99–100, 130
"Bermuda triangle", 40
Betts, Leah, 133
"big white one", 40
bingeing, on Ecstasy, 51–3
"blackjack", 40
blackouts, 9, 13, 120
"blue lagoon", 40
"blue and white", 40
body temperature, 57
    see also hyperthermia
boosting, 51
"Bouncy" E, 38–43
brain, 149
brain scans, 114
brand names, for Ecstasy, 39–41
breathing difficulties, 78
breweries, 112
"brown biscuit", 40

"Californian", 40
cannabis, 3, 9–18, 47, 53, 54, 77–8,
    80, 86–9, 99–100, 108, 117, 123,
    128–9, 134, 150
"cartoon", 40
cartoons, *see* drug leaflets
casual sex, 71–6
chemical tests, 133
chilling out, 76–84
"china split", 40
"china white", 40
cigarettes, *see* tobacco
class, 6

class A Dangerous Drugs, 1, 61, 116
classlessness, 38
class, social, 142
"clog", 40
clubbing, 9–12, 19, 22–4, 34, 37, 47,
    49, 56, 62–3, 65–71, 76–7, 93,
    120–5, 128, 134
        see also rave aspects
clubs, environment in, 135
CNS, 42–43
cocaine, 12–15, 17–18, 45, 51, 53–4,
    57, 62, 77, 86–9, 117, 122–3, 128,
    142
"coke", 28
        see also cocaine
"coke burger", 40
cola, 79
collapsing, 22
colour, and drug advice, 157–65
coming down, 79–84
concentration, problems with, 9, 12,
    16–17
condoms, 71–6
consumables, 95–6
consumption, of Ecstasy, 43–57
        frequency, 6–8
contentment, 37
crime, 9–11, 17, 96–8

dance pace, 79
dance scene, see clubbing and also
    rave aspects
death, 113–14, 129, 134
debts, 50
dehydration, 20, 25–6, 57, 76–7, 111,
    115–16
        see also hyperthermia and also
        water
delinquency, 131
dementia, 136
demography, and Ecstasy, 2–8
        and non-drug activity, 95–6
"Dennis the menace", 40
depression, 4, 9, 11, 16, 34, 60, 100,
    107–8, 116, 129–31, 134, 136–7
"diamond", 40

diarrhoea, 58
"dimples", 40
"disco biscuit", 40
"disco burger", 40
disorientation, 78
dizziness, 22–3
DJ private parties, 67
"double barrel", 40
doves, 39–43, 88
drinking fluids, see under water and
        also dehydration and also
        hyperthermia
drug adulteration, 39
drug cocktails, 21–2, 28, 53, 86–9,
    132, 135
drug dealers, 25
Drug Enforcement Agency (USA), 1
drug leaflets, 141–4, 146, 157
drug pedalling, 154
drugs, recognizing, 147, 153–4
drug rejection, 151–2

E, 24
"e130", 40
EA, 40
"eccy", 23
Ecstasy –
        addiction to, 131
        adulteration of, 115
        age and, 5, 7, 19
        and aging, 116–25, 136
        animal names for, 39–40
        as an aphrodisiac, 59
        and bad come down, 103
        bad side effects, 103
        boosting on, 51
        boredom and, 103
        brand names for, 39–42
        buying of, 61–3
        casuals and, 142
        changes over time, 41–3
        and class status, 6
        clubbers and, 142
        death on first consumption, 2
        decline in supply, 122
        demographic characteristics, 3–6

descriptive names, 39
drug dealers and, 19
education level and, 5, 8
"effect" names, 39–40
employment status and, 5–6, 8
the energy rush with, 126
erratic users of, 35–8, 44, 46, 48,
    53
experiences with, 21–4
extent of use, 1–2
ex users, 35–8, 52–3
female users, 4–5, 8
first introduction to Britain, 1
food and drink names for, 39–40
frequency of use, 34–6
friends and, 68–70
in the future, 93–5
giving up, 125–7
hassle and, 67–70
hazards information and, 116
health risks with, 148–9, 156
heavy user profile, 16–19
housing status and, 5
the hug drug, 59
illness and, 77–9, 99–102
income and, 6
information needs of users,
    111–16, 141–65
initiation routes to, 19
kidney problems with, 106
legal hazards and, 115
legalized, 91
level of use, 32
lifestyle and, 89
light user profile, 9–13
and location, 60–2, 65–7
long-term effects, 136, 147–8,
    156
the love drug, 59
main types of user, 142
male users, 4–5, 8
marital status and, 5
medium level profile, 13–15
and mood, 60–2
and mortality, 113–14, 134
music and, 70–1

need for sociability, 63–5
network of users, 28
and non-Ecstasy activities, 95–6
and other drug combinations,
    86–9
paying for, 19
people names for, 39–40
permanent cessation, 106–7
persuading other people to try,
    25–8
physical hazards, 116
place names for, 39–40
and population sampling, 2–4
price of, 48–51
and promiscuity, 74–6
psychological hazards, 116
purity of, 133
quality of, 122
questionnaires and, 2–4
quitting, 102–3
reasons for starting, 20–1
rejection of advice on, 151
reminiscences about, 116–29
role of, 85–110
safety advice on, 25–6
the scene, 91–2
a selfish drug, 27
side effects of, 147, 156
solitary consumption of, 64
sporadic moderation users, 107–8
stable users of, 35–8, 43–5, 48,
    53
stacking on, 51
temporary abstinence from,
    103–6
tolerance and, 46–8, 136
types of tablet, 38–41
types of user, 31–58
typical user, 6
typologies of use, 32–8
uses of, 59–84
vomiting and, 126
where to buy, 154
education, 8
"Eees", 24
empathy, 37

employment, 5–6, 142
entactogens, 1
erratic users, 31–110
E scene, 27
European Union, 131–2
EVA, 40
"eve", 1, 40
exercise, 134–5
exhaustion, 135, 137
exhibitions, 121
extroverted happiness, 23

fantasy, 40
fatigue, 55, 116
first aid, 78
"flatliner", 40
"flour", 39
"flying saucer", 40
"foreign E", 40
friends, 143, 145–7, 153
friendships, 125–7

Glaswegians, 5
"globe", 40
"gouchy", 41–3
"gouchy E", 38–43
"grey biscuit", 40
"greyhound", 40

hair, 4
hair testing, 131
happiness, 23, 37
hayfever, 135
headache, 78
"head fucker", 40
heart disorders, 78
"heavy", 41
hepatitis, 135
heroin, 12, 17, 22, 37, 39, 53–4, 80,
    86–9, 127, 144–6, 155
hugging, 72–4
hydration, 25–6, 57, 76–7
    see also dehydration,
        hyperthermia and also
        water
hyperthermia, 115–16, 135, 158

Ibiza, 1
illegal drugs, 130
illegal parties, 67
    see also clubbing and also raves
illness, 77–9, 99–102, 134–5
income, 6
insomnia, 12, 16–18
jellies, see temazepam

ketamine, 17, 86–9, 121, 154

language, and drug advice, 157–65
law, 133, 147, 155
leaflets, see drug leaflets
legal information, 116
"lemon and lime", 40
lifestyle, 4, 89–90, 117, 127
"little bastard", 40
liver, 135
location, and Ecstasy use, 65–8
love, 72–4
"love hearts", 40
LSD, 1, 3, 9–16, 21, 39, 53–4, 57, 70,
    77–78, 81, 83, 86–9, 93, 117, 123,
    127, 134, 148, 152, 159, 164

"M25", 40
"maddog", 40
"madman", 40
"magic white", 40
"Malcolm X", 40
"Man United", 40
MDMA, 1
media, 91–92, 111–16, 142–6
medical assistance, in clubs, 78
memory, 16, 99
memory blackouts, 121
memory failure, 4
memory problems, 9, 11–15, 116
Merck, 1
mescaline, 39, 93, 3,
    4-methylenedioxymethamphetamine,
    1
"Mickey Mouse", 40
migraines, 148
Milk of Magnesia, 57

"Milky Way", 40
"mini snowball", 40
mood, 60–61
mood swings, 9, 11– 12, 16–18, 99,
    116
muscular disorders, 78
muscular relaxation, 23
mushies, 70
mushrooms, 13–14, 16–17, 77, 86–9,
    117
    see also psilocybin
music, 69–71, 129
    see also clubbing *and also* raves
mythical side effects, of Ecstasy, 147–8

names, for Ecstasy, 39–40
    see also under specific names
native typologies, 34–6
Netherlands, 132–3
neurological problems, 135
neurotransmitter systems, 42
New Age seekers, 4
newspapers, *see under* media
"New Yorker", 40
nightclubs, *see* clubbing *and also* raves
nitrites, 3
normalised drug use, 85–100
numbness, 23

opiates, 50, 86–9, 99–100, 134
"ovals", 40
overindulgence, 108–10

paracetamol, 62
paranoia, 9, 12, 16–18, 65, 83, 101,
    116, 125, 148
parents, 143–4, 147, 149–52
Parkinson"s disease, 148
"Parma violet", 40
patterns, of Ecstasy use, 33
peer world, 132
"pellet", 40
personal maturation, 127–9
"Phase 4", 40
phoneline advice, 143, 145–6
pictures, in drug leaflets, 157–65

"pills", 39–40
"pink barrel", 40
"pink panther", 40
"pink snowball", 40
poly-drug users, 3
poppers, 14–16, 77, 86–9, 159
popular science, 114–15
posters, billboards, 143, 145
postpunk New Wavers, 4
poverty, 48
prices, 48–51
promiscuity, 74–6
psilocybin, 53–4
    see also mushrooms
psychosis, 78
"PT", 40
pubs, 66, 123, 128–9
"purple hearts", 40

rave clubs, 125
raves, 3
rave scene, 130
    see also clubbing
recommending, of Ecstasy, 25–7
"red and black", 40
"red and yellow", 40
rehydration, *see under* hydration,
    dehydration *and also* water
    and also hyperthermia
respiratory problems, 135
"rhubard and custard", 40
risk, 135, 147
risk assessment, 132
risk compensation, 133
"robin", 40
"rockets", 40
"rusk", 40

"Saddam Hussein", 40
safe drug-taking, 152
safe sex, 71–6
safety advice, 25–6
"salt and pepper", 40
schizophrenia, 148
school, 144, 146
seizures, 99

selective serotonin re-uptake
  inhibitors, 42
serotonin, 42–3, 137
serotonin systems, 136
sex, 59–61, 71–6
"SF", 40
"shamrock", 40
"shocker", 40
sleep, 22, 56, 61, 80–2, 84, 99, 126
smack, 28
    see also heroin
smacky, 41
    see also heroin
smiling, 23
smoking, *see* tobacco
"smoothies", 40
snowballing strategy, 3
"snowman", 40
sociability, 63–5
social barriers, 37
social circumstances, 60
social harassment, 67–70
social life, 35
solvents, 17, 86–9
speed, *see* amphetamines
"speedbomb", 40
squares, 39, 40–3, 88
stable users, 31–110
stacking, 51
stomach ache, 78
"strawberry", 40
stress, 135
sugar, 79
sulph (amphetamine sulphate), 45
    see also amphetamines
super dove, 40
"superman", 40
sweats, 58

tea, 79–80
television, 112, 142–4

television advertising, 144
television programmes, 144–6
temazepam, 16–17, 53–4, 80, 82,
  86–9, 118, 142
Temgesic, 17, 86–9
terms, given to Ecstasy, 39–40
theoretical sampling, 4
"tiddleiwink", 40
tobacco, 9–18, 86–9, 117, 127–8,
  130, 150
tolerance, 46–48
transmitter systems, 42
"triple X", 40
"trippy", 41
typologies, and Ecstasy, 32–8

"undergrounds", 40
unemployment, 5–6, 8
user levels, of Ecstasy, 31–110

Valium, 11, 16, 57, 82
Viagra, 123–4
"vim", 39
violence, 67–70
vision, 22, 120–1
vomiting, 22, 58
voting intentions, 95

water, 105, 135, 158
    drinking, 25–6, 76–7
    supply, 130
    see also dehydration *and also*
      hyperthermia
"wee boy", 40
weight loss, 17
"white biscuit", 40
"white caps", 40
wording, of Ecstasy leaflets, 157–65

"yellow burger", 40